C000064804

TORAH FOR TEENS

Chanukah 2007 ב״ה
To dear Brett,
Best wishes
Jeffrey M Cohen

To Gloria
with love and gratitude

And to our children:
Harvey and Lorraine
Suzanne and Keith
Judith and Bob
Lewis and Suzanne

And to our adored grandchildren:
Joel, Phil, Alex, Eliot, Abigail
Ariel, Charlotte, Maddy
Sasha, Zack, Leo
and Solomon

TORAH FOR TEENS

Growing Up Spiritually with the Weekly Sidrah

JEFFREY M. COHEN

VALLENTINE MITCHELL
LONDON • PORTLAND, OR

First published in 2008 by Vallentine Mitchell

Suite 314, Premier House, 920 NE 58th Avenue, Suite 300
112–114 Station Road,   Portland, Oregon,
Edgware, Middlesex HA8 7BJ   97213-3786

www.vmbooks.com
www.rabbijeffrey.co.uk
jeffreyandgloria@yahoo.co.uk

Copyright © 2008 Jeffrey M. Cohen

British Library Cataloguing in Publication Data
A catalogue record has been applied for

ISBN 978 0 85303 802 3 (cloth)
ISBN 978 0 85303 803 0 (paper)

Library of Congress Cataloging-in-Publication Data
A catalog record has been applied for

All rights reserved. No part of this publication may be reproduced, stored in or
introduced into a retrieval system or transmitted in any form or by any means,
electronic, mechanical, photocopying, recording or otherwise, without the prior
written permission of the publisher of this book.

Printed by Biddles Ltd, King's Lynn, Norfolk

Contents

PART TWO: SHEMOT

PART THREE: VAYIKRA

CONTENTS

PART FOUR: BEMIDBAR

PART FIVE: DEVARIM

PART SIX: SPECIAL OCCASIONS, FESTIVALS, ANNIVERSARIES AND INTERESTS

Foreword

Rabbi Dr Jeffrey Cohen is one of our master communicators. Week after week throughout a long and distinguished rabbinical career, he has expounded Torah in the classic manner, finding within the word of God for all time, the word of God for our time. A rabbi is a teacher, and a Jewish congregation is a learning community. We have been blessed in him with a teacher of insight and foresight, a true exponent of the word.

Torah for Teens is, as its title implies, a set of reflections, based on the weekly Torah portion, for young Jews in search of guidance, identity and ideals. It is a marvellous work, full of inspiration, attuned to the challenges of our time and generous in the scope and depth of its understanding.

It contains reflections on the whole range of Jewish experience from environmental, personal and social ethics to modern Jewish history, the Holocaust and the State of Israel. Rabbi Cohen brings his vast scholarly erudition to bear on all his topics, but he wears it lightly and writes simply and with grace. I recommend this work to everyone, not just teens. Each of us will find in it something new and arresting. Certainly I have.

The teenage years are a time of searching and questioning. The Hebrew word for youth, na'ar, comes from a verb that means 'to stir', and is related to the idea of awakening. It is the age at which we awake to the full possibilities of adult life, its choices and responsibilities.

The Torah itself paints some compelling portraits of young people on the threshold of greatness: Joseph and his capacity to dream dreams, Miriam and her courage in caring for her young brother Moses, and Moses himself, the fearless fighter for justice. The Torah tells these stories to signal to us, when we are young, of the greatness that awaits us if we are willing to follow our dreams and do battle on behalf of ideals.

That has not changed. It is astonishing that a faith twice as old as Christianity, three times as old as Islam, remains young and challenging. It was radical then. It is radical now. The world still needs a Jewish voice, and the Jewish people still needs greatness from its young people.

My one sadness in writing this Foreword is that Frank Cass, who encouraged and arranged for the publication of this work, is no longer with us. He was a wonderful man, a proud Jew, an ornament of our community, and one who did so much to enlarge the library of Jewish thought. May this work be a tribute to his memory.

I hope you will be as inspired by Rabbi Cohen's teachings as I have been, and may God bless you as you live the Jewish dream in a new age and write your chapter in the story of our people.

CHIEF RABBI SIR JONATHAN SACKS
London, August 2007

Introduction

This book is intended for young adults seeking to discover some religious guidance for their lives, as well as wishing to deepen their sense of Jewish identity. The Torah speaks to every age and every age group, and I have attempted to mine from each sidrah a message that is of special relevance and benefit to the young adult age group.

Each of the messages emerges from an analysis of one or more episodes in the sidrah; and this book should also serve, therefore, for an older age group as an engaging means of dipping into the weekly sidrah for some deeper insights and general instruction. The ideas expounded should also prove helpful to those called upon either to teach the weekly sidrah or to give a speech or *dvar Torah* to young people. With a minimum of adjustment, they should also be applicable to other religious occasions and to older generations.

During my forty-three years as a rabbi I inevitably attended – and continue to attend – Bar and Bat Mitzvah parties on a regular basis. When the speeches are superficial, devoid of Torah, and containing no ethical or moral ideas, neither guests nor family come away with any clear and lasting impression that they have actually been part of a religious celebration. It could be any party or banquet. Humorous speeches are entertaining, and a joke or two is certainly acceptable, but the essence of the speech should take the form of a Torah message to the young person. It is to be hoped that *Torah for Teens* will provide this in an appealing and inspirational way, serving to guide our youth through the many dilemmas and problems that will beset them during their emotionally turbulent and self-searching adolescent years, and beyond.

In the *Sim shalom* blessing of the *Amidah*, the Torah is described as *Torat chayyim*, 'The Torah of life'. This is because all human life is chronicled in it. It describes real people, saints and sinners, in the full flow of the jealousies, tensions, temptations, loves, passions and frustrations that characterized their everyday lives. The Torah shows us life in the raw: an Eve who was enticed into rebelling against God's command, and who dragged her husband down spiritually with her; a Cain who killed his brother, Abel; parents – Isaac and Rebecca – who favoured different sons; a Jacob who disguised himself as his brother, Esau, to wrest the firstborn's blessing from his father, and that same Jacob who fell in love with a beautiful girl, Rachel, who was switched by her father on the wedding night for her older and not-too-beautiful sister, Leah.

It tells us about the all-consuming jealousy of Jacob's sons for their handsome, ambitious, immensely talented, but highly self-opinionated younger brother, Joseph, who was clearly destined for greatness, culminating in their subsequent kidnap and sale of him. It describes the drunkenness of Lot and its tragic effects, and the rape of Dinah who made herself vulnerable by wandering around the countryside unaccompanied. It commiserates with the lonely, beautiful Tamar, twice-widowed daughter-in-law of Judah, who, in desperation at not having been given the husband promised to her, disguises herself as a prostitute and seduces her father-in-law in order to compromise him and force him to fulfil his promise.

The Torah describes both personal and military battles: victories and defeats, such as the tremendous inner struggles of Israel's great leader, Moses, to resolve his self-doubts and inner fears, and the battle with rivals who envied his position and who sought to exploit his areas of vulnerability. It demonstrates how those in whom he put his trust, to spy out the land of Canaan, heavily let him down by bringing a false report. It relates how his sister, Miriam, watched over him devotedly as a baby, yet, in later life, spoke out critically against him for his choice of a non-Israelite wife. And it discloses the depth of Moses' sadness that, notwith-standing the ultimate success of his mission to bring Israel to the very borders of the Promised Land, he, himself, was prevented by God from entering and witnessing the fulfilment of his life's dream. Why bad things happen to good people is underscored by the fact that the Torah starts with the punishment of banishment from the Garden of Eden for Adam's apparently minor disregard of God's instruction, and it ends with Moses' similar punishment: prevention from entering the land 'flowing with milk and honey' – a veritable 'Garden of Eden' – for, arguably, a similarly minor disregard of God's precise instructions.

These are just a few of the life-situations with which the Torah is jam-packed. And most of us – in our personal, family, profes-sional or business lives – will certainly experience something very similar to one or more of those situations.

And that is why I have put together this book, comprising mes-sages I have delivered to young people, in my former Stanmore and Canons Park community, over the past twenty years. This remains the largest Orthodox community in Europe, teeming with teens from whom I have also learned something about the changing patterns of life, and to whom I hope I have taught much about the Torah way of life. It is my sincere conviction that the Torah continues to address issues of concern and importance in our lives, and that, by exploring the messages contained in each and every sidrah, young people will find invaluable guidance as to how best to cope with their problems, how to enrich their lives, and how to find inner happiness and enhanced self-esteem.

But the Torah is not only about the problems human beings encounter in their daily lives. It is also about guiding us to become more humane, compassionate, generous-spirited, charitable, disci-plined, obedient and sensitive to the less fortunate and the less well off. It is about leading a consecrated life, a life that is based on the Torah's values and teachings. This also involves what one scholar has called 'negative ethics', which means not only learning from the biblical personalities what we should do, but also, from their mistakes, learning what not to do. This means studying their lives and learning from their shortcomings and wrongdoing. In this way we can learn something beneficial from the sinners as well as from the saints. That is also what we mean by the 'Torah of Life'.

Speaking of life, many of the young people I have addressed have had particular interests and hobbies, and special talents which they were already exploiting. Sport is, of course, high up on their order of priorities, so I have tailored messages with special reference to football, cricket and tennis, as well as to other preoccupations, such as computers, acting, art and photography. As this book targets readers as young as Bar and Bat Mitzvah, I have directed several messages to the names and significance of those occasions as well as to aspects of their celebration. I have also drawn out messages from the various festivals for those becoming Bar/Bat Mitzvah around those periods of the religious calendar.

I take this opportunity of thanking my former community of Stanmore for their unflagging interest in my various addresses to the young people, for their expressions of appreciation and criticism, as well as their frequently quite original observations. As always, I thank my dear wife, Gloria, and my beloved children and delightful grandchildren for having given me the love and joy without which the study and practice of Torah lacks a most essential ingredient. I also express my gratitude to the Chief Rabbi, Sir Jonathan Sacks, for enhancing this volume with his most illuminating foreword.

Shortly before the publication of this book, its publisher, Frank Cass, departed this life. He made a unique contribution to the field of Jewish publishing, and he will be greatly missed. I am indebted to him for having had sufficient faith in this project to undertake its publication.

JEFFREY M. COHEN
London, August 2007

Glossary

Akedah	'Binding'. Description of biblical episode of binding of Isaac (Genesis ch.22)
Amidah	'Standing Prayer'. Central prayer of every service, comprising a succession of blessings, recited standing, whose number varies according to weekday, Sabbath or festival context
Binah	'Discernment'. Ability to infer and apply Jewish law
Chochmah	'Wisdom'. Gained through study of Torah
Da'at	'Knowledge'. Denotes breadth of Torah knowledge
Eitzah	'Counsel'. Synonymous with toshi'ah
Gemara	'Completion' or 'tradition'. Name popularly applied to Talmudic commentary and supplement to the Mishnah
Haftarah	'Conclusion'. Description of passage from the prophetic literature which concludes the weekly reading from the Torah on Sabbaths and festivals
Halachah	'Religious law'. A generic term both for the entire corpus of Jewish law as well as for an individual prescription
Kaddish	'Sanctification prayer'. Affirming sanctity of God's name and kingship, recited, mainly in Aramaic, to demarcate main sections of liturgy; a variation of this prayer is also prescribed for recitation by mourners

Kavvanah	'Religious concentration'. The required state of mind for prayer and the fulfilment of religious rituals
Kohein	'Member of priestly fraternity', tracing descent to Aaron and biblical tribe of Levi. To this day entrusted with special religious functions and enjoying particular privileges and status
Lulav	'Palm branch'. Ritually waived in synagogue during festival of Succot
Maftir	'Concluding section'. Name applied to the repetition of the last few verses of the weekly Torah reading on Sabbaths and festivals; these are repeated for the one called up to read the Haftarah
Midrash	'Exposition'. Compilation of non-legal Talmudic material and exposition of ethical, moral and spiritual themes from biblical texts
Minyan	'Quorum'. Assembly of (at least) ten males over the age of 13, as required to constitute a 'congregation' for holding of public worship
Mishkan	'Sanctuary'. Portable structure serving as spiritual centre and national focus for Israelites on their Exodus from Egypt and until its replacement by the permanent Temple in Jerusalem
Mishnah	'Teaching'. Primary enumeration of Judaism's oral traditions, developed during first two centuries of the Common Era
Mitzvah	'Religious duty', 'meritorious deed'. Also refers to each of the 613 biblical laws (pl.: 'mitzvot') enumerated in the Pentateuch
Nazarite	One who bound himself by vow to observe a period of separation and abstention from physical pleasures, comforts and luxuries, such as wine and its products, and to remain unkempt, letting his hair grow wild

Omer	'Agricultural measure'. Denotes biblically pre-scribed offering of newly ripened produce to be brought to the Temple as thanksgiving; also name of seven-week period linking agricultural festivals of Pesach and Shavuot
Pirkei Avot	'Ethics of the Fathers'. Popular Mishnaic compilation of ethical maxims from Talmudic sages
Selichot	'Penitential prayers'. Recited primarily on fast days and during Ten Days of Penitence
Shemittah	'Release'. Final year of each seven-year agricultural cycle, when biblical law prescribed that land 'have rest' and go uncultivated
Shivah	'Seven'. Popular name for the seven days of home-based mourning following death of a near relative
Shmini Atzeret	'Eighth day of Solemn Assembly'. This independent festival follows on immediately after the seven days of the festival of Succot
Simchat Torah	'Rejoicing of the Law'. Follows Shmini Atzeret (in Israel it is merged with it), and celebrates the conclusion of the annual cycle of the weekly Torah reading
Succot	'Booths'. Name of festival of Tabernacles commemorating the temporary booths (Succot) which served as dwellings for the Israelites during their 40 years of journeying through the desert; also name of festival commemorating that aspect of the Exodus
Tefillin	'Phylacteries'. Leather boxes containing four biblical passages referring to this ritual obligation, secured to the arm and head by means of leather straps and worn during the weekday morning services
Tevunah	'Perception'. Denotes quality of incisiveness in Torah study

Torah	'Instruction'. Variously denotes Five Books of Moses, body of religious law and lore, or any religious exposition
Toshi'ah	'Advice'. Synonym for Eitzah
Yahrzeit	'Anniversary'. Solemn commemoration of anniversary of death of close relatives

PART ONE
BEREISHIT

CHAPTER ONE

Bereishit:
The name Adam

The sidrah Bereishit describes the creation of the first man, and the name 'Adam' that was given to him. Our sages tell us that this name can mean either of two diametrically opposite qualities. The first associates the name with the word *adamah*, meaning 'earth, ground'. Alternatively, it may be derived from the word *demut*, which means 'image', and refers specifically to the divine image in which man was created (Genesis 1: 27).

We can set our sights in either direction: either as low as the *adamah*, the earth, focusing exclusively on our physical needs and pleasures, making us little different from the lower forms of nature who are also preoccupied with what the earth can produce for their pleasure and survival. Or we can set our sights on heaven and attempt to discover the *demut*, the 'image' of God as reflected in man. It is that which provides us with our potential for kindness and sympathy, nobleness, creativity, artistry and sensitivity to higher causes and challenges.

The *demut*, the divine image, can sometimes shine through even in the midst of the deepest moral depravity. This was exemplified by the lives and activities of men such as Oskar Shindler and Raoul Wallenberg who defied the Nazis to rescue countless Jews. The name of another such hero, De Sousa Mendes, a Portuguese diplomat, was revealed some twenty years ago. He also issued visas to Jews and others on the Nazi death list, in defiance of the instructions of his superiors in the British embassy in Lisbon. His action enabled some 30,000 people to flee in the nick of time, before the

Nazis sealed the borders. As a result of his refusal to obey his immoral orders, Mendes was dismissed from his post, and was deprived of his livelihood and his pension. He ended his days in a lodging-house for the destitute and forgotten! Acts of such self-lessness and heroism testify to the existence of the *demut*, the image of God in man.

But too often that heaven-directed urge is so deeply hidden within our subconscious that we ourselves may be totally unaware that we possess it, and how to express it. There is often a high price to be paid for responding to its call, especially in an age when all around us are betraying its existence and behaving as if man was no more than the sum of his physical parts.

Men who endangered their own lives to save countless others, such as Raoul Wallenberg and De Sousa Mendes, were clearly acutely aware of the awesome responsibility which that image of God within them imposed, even to the extent of having to endanger their lives in the cause of truth, mercy and justice.

The challenge of the name *Adam* is to strive to reflect the *demut*, the divine image, in everything we do, to be prepared to make sacrifices in the cause of justice, honour and truth, and for our people and our homeland, Israel, and to keep far from any behaviour that we sense instinctively will propel us earthward to the arena of *adamah*, the mere satisfaction of our 'earthly' desires and our physical appetite.

CHAPTER TWO

Bereishit:
Learning from Adam's mistakes

The Torah was never intended to be a science textbook, and its account of the Creation is obviously no more than the broadest statement of the order in which the earliest organisms evolved, from simple, single cells to more complex formations, from insects to man.

The story of that first man, Adam, is most intriguing. He was placed into the Garden of Eden, and given the solemn command, *le'ovdah ul'shomrah*, 'to tend and protect it'. He was to enjoy all its fruits, with the exception of two: the fruit of the tree of life and of the tree of the knowledge of good and evil. The fruit of the first tree would give man immortality; the fruit of the second tree would transform him from a being programmed to do only good into one with a knowledge of, and inclination towards, evil.

Adam disregarded God's mission. Not only did he not protect the matchless trees, but he even set about plundering the fruit of the tree of knowledge in order to experience good and evil. The punishment imposed on him, banishment from the Garden, may seem harsh, but it is one that our generation may well sympathize with. Like Adam, we have also squandered so many of the world's natural resources that we now have to undertake emergency conservation and recycling measures to safeguard our planet for future generations.

Adam clearly could not be trusted to do that, so banishment was inevitable.

And his offspring have suffered the consequences of that exile ever since, in the interminable battles we have had to wage with nature to extract a livelihood and to survive its harshest natural elements, such as earthquakes, tsunamis and famine. We have also found ourselves in conflict with nature when we set out to exploit her riches, as in the struggle to mine her minerals, destroy her rainforests and pollute her rivers with industrial waste.

One of the many lessons of the Garden of Eden episode is that man's task should be *le'ovdah ul'shomrah* – 'to guard and protect' whatever we have: be it nature's gifts, be it our way of life, our ethical and moral values, our religious heritage, or our family relationships.

Our society seems to think that progress must involve change; that pleasure can only be gained by sweeping away the familiar, comfortable and cosy things, and constantly replacing them with a more modern version, even if that entails squandering our natural resources. We hardly have time to enjoy what we have acquired today before we are being told, by alluring and sophisticated publicity, that those who are truly 'with-it' have already discarded our model for one that is much closer to the cutting-edge of fashion or technological progress.

We may suppose that we have Adam to blame for that, since he was the first to reject God's call to him to conserve and protect the environment and the way of life that he had inherited. He was not content with the blessings God had given him. Instead, he preferred to experiment, to taste fruits whose effects he could not possibly have anticipated. God had called it, 'the tree of the knowledge of good and evil'. Adam gambled on its fruit being 'good' for him, and he conveniently ignored the reference to evil. Perhaps that was not surprising, since he had hitherto never experienced evil.

Every God-given soul, every mind, every personality, is unique, as is the potential that invests us all. But, like Adam and Eve, no one seems satisfied with who they are, with how they look, with what they have achieved, with the direction in which their life seems to be taking them. And that dissatisfaction lies at the root of the problems that so many people take to psychiatrists and counsellors these days. They do not appreciate the Garden of Eden they are living in, or their ability to transform their own lives into something approximating that idyllic state. This can truly be achieved by doing what God told Adam to do, namely, *le'ovdah* – 'to work' – on themselves and on their relationships – *ul'shomrah*, 'and to preserve' – protect and be satisfied with the blessings they already enjoy.

CHAPTER THREE

Noach:
Mixed blessings

The sidrah Noach describes the flood that devastated mankind as a punishment for its depravity. It is a fact that anything in excess, even blessings and pleasures, can be transformed easily into a source of pain and suffering. We know that this is so in the case of drugs and alcohol. The story of Noach and the Flood demonstrates how this was also true in the case of water.

Water is vital to our physical health. It is also the largest component of the human body. It is essential for agriculture and in the manufacturing process, if not the ingredients, of most of the goods we use and the food and drink we enjoy. But when nature hurls it at us, in the form of floods, tidal waves and tsunamis, then its effects are devastating.

Noach's wicked generation learnt that to their cost. They exploited God's blessings without moral responsibility or a sense of proportion; and God punished them measure for measure, by employing one of His most precious blessings, that of water, in a disproportionate measure.

Interestingly, the previous sidrah, Bereishit, provides the identical cautionary tale. God planted a garden, but when Adam became greedy, and demanded more than his fair share of fruit from that garden, its blessing became his undoing.

The genius of the Hebrew language conveys this teaching through the double meaning of the word berachah. In addition to the usual meaning of 'blessing', the verb barech also occurs in the sense of 'to curse'. The wife of Job tells her pious husband, who can no longer bear his pain and punishment, *barekh Elokim umut*, 'curse God and die!' (Job 2: 9) The same word for two diametrically opposite ideas! The same blessing can, if abused, become a curse.

The message is that with blessing comes responsibility. The Hebrew word for 'knee', *berech*, is at the core of the word for a blessing, *berachah*. When we are endowed with blessings, we must, metaphorically, get down on our knees. We must display humility, acknowledge how undeserving we are, and how fortunate therefore to be the recipients of all God's goodness. And that is why we make blessings over every one of God's gifts.

Eve was not content with her abundant blessings. She hankered after what she did not possess. And the way she reported to the serpent what God had commanded her husband was very revealing. She alleged that God had said: *mipri eitz ha-gan nocheil*, 'we may eat of all the fruits' – except for the one that is off limits. Eve implied that God had given them a concession, namely that if they *wished* they were at liberty to indulge their craving.

But that was not, in fact, what God had said. His words were, *Mikol eitz ha-gan achol tocheil*, 'You *must surely* eat of all the fruits'. God actually gave them a mitzvah here, a command, to eat and enjoy the blessing of all the other trees. Had Eve appreciated that to enjoy God's blessings is a mitzvah, perhaps she would have eaten them with a greater sense of privilege, pleasure and humility. Perhaps, then, she would not have so desperately longed for the solitary tree that was denied to her.

So the message that emerges from this sidrah is to be ever grateful for all the blessings we enjoy, to thank God for them and to appreciate that, like the blessing of water which turned into the curse of a Flood, blessings of any kind, if not wisely and constructively used, can also bring pain, suffering and ruin.

So let us use our blessings wisely, and thank God for them every day of our lives. Let us *be* a blessing, *count* our blessings, *share* our blessings, and continue throughout our life to study and observe our Torah – the source of all our blessing.

CHAPTER FOUR

Lech Lecha:
A blueprint for Jewish history

The sidrah Lech Lecha relates the main episodes in the life of Abram, beginning with the command that, at 75 years of age, he should leave his country of Chaldea, adjacent to Babylon, and travel to an as yet unknown destination in order that his people may become a great nation. He does as he is told, and arrives at Canaan. But the years roll on, and still there are no offspring, let alone a great nation. There follows a bitter famine, necessitating a further uprooting of Abram and Sarah from Canaan and an exile to Egypt.

Our rabbis were not slow to detect the significance of those journeys, between Mesopotamia, or Babylon, and Israel and Egypt: the precise axis of future exiles for the offspring of Abram, who were exiled to Egypt, before returning to Israel. Then, in 586 BCE, they were taken captive into Babylon before returning to build the second Temple in Israel. However, within a few hundred years they once again came under the rule of the Ptolemies, the rulers of Egypt, who had invaded Israel. Not surprisingly, our rabbis see, mirrored in the life and the journeying of Abra(ha)m, the future fate of the Jewish people. Hence their maxim, *ma'aseh avot siman lebanim*, 'the history of the fathers foreshadows that of their children', or, as we would say, 'history repeats itself'. That is certainly the case with Jewish history.

Let us look at some further ways in which the fate of Abram foreshadowed what was to happen to his offspring. He was told to pick up his roots and make for a distant land, *asher arehka*, 'which I shall show you' (Genesis 12: 1). The precise destination is with-

10

held, just as it was for generations of future Jewish refugees who had to flee their host countries, not knowing where they would be granted refuge and would be able to put down fresh roots. Abram feared that the Egyptians would kill him in order to seize his beautiful wife. That foreshadowed an edict later issued by another King of Egypt regarding the fate of the Hebrew children. The boys were to be killed – thrown into the Nile – while the girls were to be seized as future wives for the Egyptians.

When Abram and Sarah, through God's intervention, managed to leave Egypt, and return to Canaan, their troubles were by no means over: Abram immediately fell out with his nephew, Lot. Rabbinic tradition explains the dispute on the basis of the standards of honesty of Lot's shepherds having been unacceptable to Abram who insisted, therefore, that he and his nephew part company. The fact that Lot chose to go and live in the corrupt area of Sodom, while Abram lived in Canaan, also foreshadowed the future history of Israel when, on the death of King Solomon, his kingdom was divided into two: an idolatrous northern kingdom of Israel, or Samaria, and a southern kingdom of Judah, or Judea, that remained loyal to God. Like the separation of Abram and his nephew, so the Jewish nation of that first commonwealth, that should have retained its sense of family unity and religious integrity, instead became divided and weakened, and ultimately succumbed to invasion and enslavement.

When he subsequently heard that his estranged nephew, Lot, had been captured in a battle, Abram risked his own life by joining in with an independent battle that he sensed might afford him the chance to rescue his kith and kin. Does this not also foreshadow the Jewish sense of collective responsibility which our beloved State of Israel has so inspirationally demonstrated? Israel has pulled off many most daring exploits in order to rescue endangered Jews from Yemen, Ethiopia and Arab countries, including the amazing Entebbe raid to rescue a planeload of Jews who had been hijacked there. Israel's greatest achievement was the behind-the-scenes diplomatic efforts to rescue millions of Soviet Jews. Abram pointed the way. His compassion, sense of mission and readiness to sacrifice was an inspiration and model for all his offspring.

To return to Abram: while still awaiting the fulfilment of God's promise to make him a great nation, he had a dream wherein God says, *Al tiyra Avram anochi magen lach secharcha harbeh me'od* — 'Do not fear, Abram. I am protecting you; your reward will be very great!' (Genesis 15: 1) Any lesser man, bearing in mind that this was a dream, and one can get away with far more in a dream than in reality, would have said,

> God, you really have a great sense of humour! You promised me years ago that if I moved to Canaan I would become a blessing. But what did I get? Nothing but trouble, strife, exile, and a close shave with death. And as for the great nation that I was supposed to become — some joke! You did not even give me one child! So much for my great reward!

But Abram did not reply in that way. He did not criticize God, however justifiable that may have been. He merely and gently alluded to God's former promise, saying, *Hashem Elokim mah titein liy* — 'But, Lord God, rewards matter little to me. After all, I have no children!' (verse 2) What an amazingly gentle and moderated reminder to God!

That is how Abram bore his trials and tribulations. He had faith in God. He embodied what Maimonides was later to codify as the great Jewish capacity for patience — *V'af al piy sheyitmahme'a im kol zeh achakeh loh kol zeman sheyavo* — 'And even if God's destiny for us is delayed, nevertheless I shall wait patiently for it, for whenever it shall come.'

And that is what we Jews have been doing for 2,000 years: experiencing countless exiles, suffering unspeakable horrors, having our Jewish world divided, with Jews detached from each other across the globe. We also, like Abram, have been rescuing our brethren whenever we could, never becoming impatient, never losing our faith in God's promise that one day our people would be reunited, with Israel as our national focus and inspiration.

The personality of Abram is the blueprint for all the faith, patience, inner strength, determination and optimism that characterize our people. It was the preliminary sketch from which the rich, dramatic and complex canvas of Jewish history was later to be painted.

CHAPTER FIVE

Vayeira:
Religious enthusiasm

The sidrah Vayeira begins with a description of Abraham's act of warm hospitality which became the hallmark of the Jewish people. His welcome to three desert travellers to come in to his home, and to eat and refresh themselves, is hailed as the classical example of his love of humankind.

But there is a problem here. After all, in last week's sidrah, we read of Abraham returning from the great battle in which nine local kings were embroiled. His participation ensured victory, to the extent that he was able to rescue his nephew, Lot, who had been previously captured by the enemy. As Abraham was wearily wending his way home across the desert plains, no doubt physically and mentally exhausted, we are told, *Umalki-Zedek melech shalem hotzi lechem va-yayin*, that 'Malki-Zedek the king of Salem, a priest of the Most High God, brought out to him bread and wine' (Genesis 14: 18). He then proceeded to give Abraham a blessing.

So we see that Abraham was not the first to display hospitality and concern for wayfarers. Indeed, some may argue that it was the example of Malki-Zedek that inspired Abraham to do likewise! Why then is Abraham, and not Malki-Zedek, held up as the paragon and embodiment of the virtue of hospitality?

I would suggest that there was a world of difference between the two acts. Significantly, Malki-Zedek did not invite Abraham home. *Hotzi lechem va-yayin*, 'he brought out bread and wine'. Malki-Zedek clearly also believed in the one God, and seems to have established a religious community of which he designated himself 'the priest'. This term is suggestive of a select and closed religious fraternity which regarded outsiders as a source of impurity. This may well explain why he kept Abraham at arm's length, making sure that Abraham stayed on the road, offering him no invitation to return to his place to wash and refresh himself and to relax his exhausted limbs. What a contrast to Abraham, who went out and brought the three men home, extending to them a full and warm hospitality, inviting them to bathe and take a nap under the shade of his trees.

This contrast is also marked in respect of the food that they both offered. Malki-Zedek gave Abraham bread and wine, a rather strange gesture when we consider that it is water that is needed by a desert traveller, not wine! Bread and water is what Abraham later provided for Hagar and Ishmael before they left for their long journey through the desert (Genesis 21: 14). Bread and wine would hardly be relished by someone who had had no access to wells of fresh water for days! Compare, then, Malki-Zedek's meagre fare with Abraham's banquet of freshly baked cakes, of the most tender steaks from a calf he personally had selected, accompanied by milk and curd. What a contrast! Malki-Zedek's was barely a finger snack. Abraham's was a banquet.

Thirdly, in Christian theology, Malki-Zedek, a priest-king, is regarded as a saviour, the inspiration for the founder of their faith. The fact that he served bread and wine, which later became a basic religious symbol in Christianity, suggests that his gift to Abraham was meant to be understood more as a religious ritual, a symbolic food, than a meal to be enjoyed. According to this reading of the passage, Malki-Zedek came out to bless Abraham, a fellow worshipper of the one God, and offered him the bread and wine merely as a token of religious fellowship, not as a demonstration of hospitality. And hence it is Abraham, and not Malki-Zedek, who is justly acclaimed for his unique hospitality to wayfarers.

The enthusiasm and personal involvement with which Abraham and Malki-Zedek performed their respective acts is also enlightening. Malki-Zedek 'brought out' bread and wine. Abraham, on the other hand, no sooner had he seen the men on the horizon, va-yar va-yarotz likratam, 'ran to meet them from the

14

entrance of his tent'. Note that this was an elderly man who, just three days earlier, had performed circumcision on himself, and must have been rather sore and weak. Yet he bowed down before the travellers and begged them not to pass by, but to honour him by accepting his hospitality.

As if that were not enough, *Vay'maheir Avraham ha-ohelah el Sarah*, 'Abraham rushed into Sarah's tent', and excitedly gave her the good news that they had visitors. So anxious was he that the way-farers' desire to arrive at their destination promptly should not prevent them from accepting his hospitality that he gave Sarah a rather curt instruction: *Mahariy*, 'hurry! – get baking!'

But Sarah was not offended; and the text conveys clearly the sense of excitement and the feverish activity building up in their home. Abraham positively 'raced' out of Sarah's tent: *v'el ha-bakar ratz Avraham*, 'Abraham ran to [select the best] calf' – and delivered it to his cook to prepare. *Va-yikach chem'ah v'chalav*, 'and he then went off to select the dairy fare'; *va-yitein lifneihem*, 'and he set it before them'. He did not delegate the task to a servant: *Vehu omeid aleihem*, 'and he stood by, waiting upon them while they ate'.

What a difference between the two respective acts. Malki-Zedek had a ritual to perform, and he went through the motions of performing it. Abraham went through the e-motions! The opportunity to offer hospitality was positively exciting for him. His enthusiasm literally leaps off the page of the Chumash.

This is how Abraham fulfilled every mission, both the pleasurable ones like this, as well as the awesome and testing ones, such as the mission to take his son, Isaac, to the *Akedah*. He knew what God expected of him. And everything he did, in response to God's expectation, was done with a sense of privilege, duty, love and passion. This is the message and challenge of this fascinating sidrah.

CHAPTER SIX

Chayei Sarah:
Learning from both
saints and sinners

The great bible commentator, Rashi, asks why the Torah – which is principally a law book – included the book of Genesis which contains simple stories from the lives of our earliest ancestors, the fathers and mothers of the Jewish people. Why, he asks, did it not commence with chapter 12 of Exodus, which inaugurates Torah law by describing all the requirements for the first, and subsequent, Passover celebrations? (see Rashi on Genesis 1: 1)

I believe that the Torah is actually making a very profound statement. The book of Genesis details the halting attempts of early man to develop a moral and ethical conscience. It shows how men, such as those of the generation of the Flood or of the Tower of Babel, behaved under the influence of an underdeveloped moral conscience. Stories such as the murder of Abel by his brother Cain, and the selling of Joseph into slavery in Egypt by his older brothers, indicate the level of brutality to which men were capable of descending in the absence of moral or ethical restraint.

The book of Genesis serves as a warning to our generation, which is also, in many respects, heartless and violent, of what dangers lie in store for such a society. Secondly, it teaches that moral responsibility and ethical concern must be in place before people are receptive to receiving laws. That is why, in addition to all the wicked people whose deeds are chronicled in the book of Genesis, we also have the stories of the righteous founders of our nation – the matriarchs and patriarchs – who helped to banish evil and teach new values of goodness and charitableness to an infant mankind.

That is what Judaism is all about. It is not some vague or idealistic philosophy; it is a blueprint for an honest, caring society, where people's word is their bond, and where no one takes any unfair advantage of another. Some may, indeed, regard that as an idealistic philosophy, but Judaism insists that that has to be the basis of any civilized society, and that spirituality and the religious life cannot begin to flourish where there are no basic ethics and morals.

In this sidrah's account of Abraham's business dealings with the Hittite prince, Ephron (Genesis 23: 1–20), we have a profile of both proper and improper conduct. When Abraham sent his initial request to Ephron, through the Hittite townsfolk, that he would like to purchase the cave of Machpelah on the edge of Ephron's estate for a burial plot, Ephron grasped the opportunity to pass himself off as a most gracious and generous leader who could not possibly accept money, especially from a 'prince of God' who had only recently honoured them by taking up residence in their midst. Hence, when Ephron was next seated at the head of the city council, surrounded by 'all those entering his city', he called out in a loud voice to Abraham, 'No, my lord, hear me. I give you the whole field and the cave within it. In the presence of the children of my people, I hereby give it to you' (verse 11). But Abraham replied, in an equally loud voice, so that everyone might hear, 'Please listen carefully, I must give the price of the field. Take it from me' (verse 13).

Ephron did not require much persuasion, and he immediately named his price. Having originally publicly insisted that he would not take any money, Ephron now reveals his true colours, whispering to Abraham, 'What is four hundred shekel to men like us? Bury your dead' (verse 15).

Well, if we wish to know the value of 400 shekel in those days, we have a contemporary record, in the form of Hammurabi's Code, which tells us that the average annual wage for a worker was about seven shekels. And that is how the generous Ephron was 'giving the field away' to Abraham! 'Letting it go' at a 'knock-down' price, equivalent to over fifty-five years' wages – the salary of a man for his entire working life! Some generosity! Some business ethics!

Ephron falsely constructed for himself a reputation of being a man of integrity, concern, kindness, helpfulness and a generous supporter of the cause of the stranger in society, when all along he was craftily exploiting the opportunity in private for gross extortion. And this is the sense of the Hebrew, *beiniy uveincha*, '[Let's keep this] between me and you! No one needs to know our business!' (verse 15)

Ephron symbolized those whose public and private persona are quite different. He was a two-faced rogue who used people. Abraham, on the other hand, was the personification of goodness, kindness, honesty and diplomacy. However outraged Abraham must have been, he did not utter a word: *Vayishma Avraham el Ephron*, 'And Abraham listened to Ephron' (verse 16). Abraham's silence spoke volumes. He truly was a prince; and not only did he pay the price without so much as a word, but he also paid it in coinage described as *oveir lasocheir*, 'that could be turned over immediately to a merchant'. That is, silver coins that were in uniform and convenient size and weight, and that no one, in those days, would insist on examining to determine their silver composition and reliability. What a contrast between the Israelite and the Hittite business ethics.

We often learn as much from the biblical rogues as we do from the righteous. From the rogues we learn what *not* to do; from the righteous we learn what to do. From Ephron we learn never to give the impression that we are more righteous and more deserving of praise than is truly the case.

Our modern world is a place of camouflage, where image rather than essence is regarded as all-important. We have an entire industry, linked to advertising and public relations, geared to making products appear more alluring and valuable to the gullible consumer than they really are. Decades ago it would have been called 'misrepresentation'. Today it is called 'marketing'. That was the approach of Ephron, not of Abraham.

From Abraham we learn the meaning of sacrifice, of truth, of integrity, of *chesed*, kindness and consideration for the feelings and the reputation of others – even of an Ephron. We learn when to hold our peace, and when to speak out, with courage and conviction, especially on issues that affect our society and our people.

In brief, the message of this sidrah is to learn from all people and all situations: to learn whom to trust and whom not to trust, when to make a fuss and when to hold one's peace, whom to embrace as a friend and whom to keep at arm's length.

CHAPTER SEVEN

Chayei Sarah:
Moving on into adulthood

The sidrah Chayei Sarah opens with a description of the sum total of the years of Sarah's life, but the way it expresses that total is rather cumbersome. It states that she lived *meah shanim v'es-rim shanah v'sheva shanim*, 'one hundred years and twenty years and seven years' (Genesis 23: 1). Our commentators try to explain why that number is divided up and compartmentalized in that particular way. Rashi explains it as implying that at one hundred she was as free of sin as she was at 20, and that at 20 she possessed the (complexion and) beauty of a 7-year-old.

But the fact that the Torah also divides up the years of the lives of Abraham and Ishmael in that same compartmentalized manner suggests to us that it comes rather to convey some more general aspect of life's division into three main periods of transition and opportunity. These may be divided into the periods of birth to childhood (0–7 years), childhood to maturity (7–20 years), and, finally, maturity, through prime, to old age (20–100 years).

In the case of Sarah, that division of her life may serve to underline the fact that each stage was lived and enjoyed to the full, and that she utilized every opportunity for personal development that each stage of her life presented.

The division of Abraham's life into three periods of 'one hundred years and seventy years and five years' (Genesis 25: 7) may be explained in terms of his spiritual growth. The 'five years' may relate to the earliest period of his life when he was still under the idolatrous influence of his father, Terach. The second period (5–70

20

years) witnessed his search for and discovery of God and the development of his relationship with him; and the final one hundred years spanned the account of his activities, struggles and religious mission, as recorded in the Torah.

The division of Ishmael's life into three periods of 'one hundred years and thirty years and seven years' (Genesis 25: 17) may also be a pointer to the main stages of his life. The 'seven years' may refer to the first seven years of his life, spent under the spiritually nurturing influence of his father, Abraham. The next 'thirty years' denotes a period characterized by rebellion against his parental values and a slide into moral degeneracy, followed by a long and final period ('one hundred years') which, according to the Midrash (quoted by Rashi on Genesis 25: 9), was spent in repentance and reconciliation.

Most of our children enjoy a happy childhood within a cocoon of love, indulgence and generosity provided by doting parents, grandparents and other close relatives. But they must move on from the stage of childhood into the stage of youth. In that period they are expected to gain in maturity in order to prepare themselves for the responsibilities and trials of beckoning adulthood, and to grow spiritually in order to develop the faith and courage to overcome life's many trials and temptations.

There are too many young people who are unwilling to grow up or accept their adult Jewish duties and responsibilities. Many teenagers are indistinguishable in that respect from 7-year-olds. They make their own needs and childish pleasures the sole objective of their lives. By the time they have reached 20, too many are still immature Jewishly and have little real comprehension of their own history, faith, culture, or the problems confronting young people of their own age in Israel. Tragically, a high proportion of those in the final period of their lives look back and realize that they have never moved on, but have remained permanently locked into the stage they occupied and the self-interests they pursued when they were 20.

Though the years and decades have moved on, they remained behind, never exploiting the manifold opportunities that life and Judaism offered them, to expand their mind and horizons, to contribute to the community and to society, never learning, growing or enriching the lives of others, never sharing their prosperity with, or making sacrifices for, the less fortunate, never offering comfort or spreading love beyond their immediate family and circle of friends.

The message of the three stages of life is that we must never stand still, because that means stagnation. We must be ever ready to progress and to explore the challenges, possibilities and responsibilities that are offered to us all as we progress through life's various stages. We must also ensure that we continually grow in maturity and sensitivity, avoiding the pitfalls and temptations of the past, but forever learning from and building on the experience we have accumulated along the way.

CHAPTER EIGHT

Toldot:
Who is the real 'me'?

This week's sidrah finds Rebecca in a physically and emotionally distressed state. She is pregnant with twins, and is experiencing a most unusual inner turbulence, as if the two foetuses were engaged in a mortal battle with each other.

She has an inner foreboding that this foreshadows a life – possibly even a future history – of conflict between these two children and their offspring. (Esau, in our tradition, represents the Christian world. His other name, Edom, is also a symbol of Rome, which in the fourth century CE recognized Christianity as the official religion of the Roman Empire. The long history of Church-inspired oppression of the Jews, culminating in the Holocaust, more than confirmed Rebecca's worst fears.)

The Midrash attempts to explain the precise cause of the struggle within Rebecca's womb. It suggests that, when she passed by a meeting-place of an idolatrous cult, Esau violently struggled to exit the womb in order to participate in the idolatrous practice. When she passed by a place dedicated to the worship of the One God, on the other hand, Jacob desperately sought to push his brother out of the way so that he could emerge to pray (see Rashi on Genesis 25: 22).

This upset Rebecca emotionally. She could not comprehend how a righteous woman like her could possibly be carrying two children so spiritually in conflict. Had she lived in modern times, and understood something about inherited genes, she would have appreciated that this could well be attributable to the fact that she was the daughter of the wicked Betuel, and that her brother, Laban, similarly did not have a spark of spirituality in him. It was very possible, therefore, that, while one of the twins, Jacob, could have inherited the noble character and religious sensitivity of her husband, Isaac, the other one, Esau, could have been invested with the genetic characteristics of her own family.

But Rebecca was totally confused, and sank into a depression. 'If this is what is happening', she moaned, 'lamah zeh anochi? – Who exactly am I?' (Genesis 25: 22). Now, it is difficult to know the precise meaning of the latter three, disjointed, Hebrew words. Literally they mean, 'why (lamah), this (zeh), I (anochi)'. It would seem that she was, indeed, brooding especially over the evil nature of Esau, and attempting to make sense of the fact that part of her own inner being – her anochi, which she had undoubtedly passed on to him – must also be wicked.

But the question that Rebecca asks herself here can have a much wider application. It is truly a question that everyone should ask whenever they seem to be doing something that is out of character, when allowing their weaker nature to gain the upper hand or when giving in to temptation. The question is, lamah zeh anochi – 'Why this I?' 'Why have I descended to this low level? Why am I behaving like someone who is so different to the real "me"? What must I do to allow that real "me" – the good, kind, responsible, honest, moral "me" – to re-surface?'

Discovering the real 'me' is an extremely important, and sometimes very difficult, exercise, for young people in particular. This is because it is natural for them to seek to adopt different 'images' to show to the outside world. Those images are often based on the nature of the people they have created as their role models: people whose looks, style, magnetic personality and reputed wealth they only wished they possessed.

Some girls dress provocatively in order to attract the attention of boys. They naively believe that they will win real admiration, respect and love in that way. What they are really doing is diverting the attention of the opposite sex away from the real 'me', the real person, the real personality. They are, in effect, making the statement that it is their body, not their individuality, character or qualities that is on display. This may be compared to a shop that sold rare items, but whose window displayed things that one might buy at any number of other stores. It is the same with young men who resort to loutish behaviour in order to draw attention to themselves. They only demonstrate thereby how devoid of real appeal they are, how lacking in other desirable qualities, how unable they are to gain attention by the interest of their conversation, the liveliness and sharpness of their wit, the attractiveness of their personality.

The word 'personality' is defined as 'that quality that makes a being personal'. There is a profound message here for young people, namely that it is the person and the personality that distinguishes an individual from all those around. Indeed, the personality generally survives long after the body's looks have declined. It is the source of our liveliness and character. It is the mirror of our inner being and our soul.

So the question every young person should ask is, 'Why am I trying to be a clone of someone else when I have within me that which is absolutely unique? Why should I borrow someone else's image when God has given me my own unique and precious "self"? Why should I throw away my own diamond, and then go borrowing someone else's?'

The message to our youth is to follow Rebecca's lead, and to ask themselves that important question, *lamah zeh anochi*, 'Who is the real "me"?' When they have discovered the answer to that question, they will have discovered true confidence and lasting happiness.

CHAPTER NINE

Vayeitzei:
The age of Bat Mitzvah

The Bat Mitzvah/Bat Chayil ceremonies have come late on the Jewish ritualistic scene, and it is only over the past forty years that they have been formally celebrated in many synagogues. Indeed, there are still rabbis who object to holding a synagogue ceremony to mark this occasion. They argue that, as women do not have any special role within the synagogue service, it is positively misleading to launch a young girl into Jewish womanhood in such an artificial manner. (I suppose the same could be said for having a chupah in a synagogue, as that bride will never again have the privilege of standing in the centre of the shul or on the bimah, in such close proximity to the rabbi and chazan, when they are reciting blessings.)

That is not to say that the age of female religious responsibility – 12 years of age – was not recognized. Indeed, it was. The Talmud (Kidushin 16b) already referred to it some 1,800 years ago in the same context as it recorded the age of male responsibility at 13. It was just that, because in Orthodoxy only the males have a duty to perform daily prayer and other time-related religious duties – women being free to attend to the many pressing needs of their homes and families – the result was that the synagogue became largely a male preserve. Thus, a certain inhibition was felt on the part of young women to have a high-profile celebration in the full glare of the community. However, the equality that women gained during the twentieth century changed many perceptions, and Modern or Centrist Orthodoxy is largely defined now in terms of its enlightened attitude to the pursuit of women's spirituality and their growing role in synagogue life.

Becoming Bar or Bat Mitzvah means more than asserting one's enhanced religious status and privileged position as an adult member of the Jewish community. It is the attainment of an age when one is regarded as mature enough to understand the importance of serving the community and of putting the greater good before the pursuit of one's own narrow interests.

Membership of the Jewish religious community is not extended to children because a child is naturally self-centred. What 'I want' is the prime objective of children. They cannot be expected to appreciate that without a protective, content, supportive and safe community around them, their own position and future is unsafe and uncertain. They cannot be expected, therefore, to think and care about, and work for, enterprises beyond themselves. Alas, there are also too many adults who never mature in that respect, and live only for themselves, their own pleasure, their own immediate family's well-being.

In the sidrah *Vayetzei* this idea is vividly conveyed in the story of Jacob's dream of the ladder joining heaven and earth, with the angels going up and down. The question is asked why Jacob only had that unique spiritual disclosure at the stage of his life when he was on the run from his brother, Esau, who was seeking to murder him for having seized his birthright? Why did he not have that vision earlier, when still under his parents' roof?

The answer is contained in the words Jacob uses on waking up from his dream: 'Surely God is in this place' – *v'anochiy loh yadatiy* – 'And I never knew it' (Genesis 28: 16). Now, the word *v'anochiy*, 'And I', is superfluous here. Jacob could simply have said, *v'loh yadatiy*, which, without the *v'anochiy*, also means, 'And I never knew it!'

But Jacob's use of that extra word is significant. For the phrase *v'anochiy loh yadatiy* can also mean 'I did not know *anochiy*', that is, 'I ceased to know *myself*'. I have only had God's presence revealed to me now that I have abandoned my preoccupation with *anochiy*, with 'myself', my own needs, desires and ambitions.

As long as Jacob lived in the family home, he was doted on by his mother in particular, with all his needs provided, with few responsibilities, focusing exclusively on his *anochiy*, his own creature comforts, not even going out to hunt for food for the rest of the family, as did Esau. In that situation there was no way he was going to worry about the needs of others, to the extent that he would be able to fulfil his destiny to become a patriarch of a nation and the founder of twelve tribes. It was only when he was forced to forget about home comforts and material needs and flee from his home that he began to put life into proper perspective. Only then did a sense of destiny dawn on him. Only then did he think about higher and nobler ideals, greater and holier objectives.

Achein yesh Hashem bamakom hazeh – 'Surely God's presence is in this place', said Jacob. 'Now I understand the message of the revelation of the ladder stretching from earth to heaven, of the many spiritual rungs that human beings are capable of scaling, and the proximity to heaven that can be experienced – *v'anochiy loh yadatiy* – when one no longer cares about *anochiy*, one's own narrow and selfish comforts and ambitions.'

And that is why religious maturity is viewed as occurring at the age of 12 for girls and 13 for boys. That is the age when they are expected to liberate themselves from the childish perception that everything revolves around them alone. That is the age when Judaism believes young people are already developing a greater sensitivity towards the religious life, the common good, and the needs of the less fortunate in our community. Since girls at that period are already developing their 'maternal instinct', and concern for the future lives that they are to nurture and bring into the world, their maturing process kicks in earlier than that of boys. Hence the Bat Mitzvah at 12 years of age.

CHAPTER TEN

Vayishlach:
The Jewish attitude to violence

The sidrah Vayishlach is one that rewards close study because of the many important lessons contained in it. It relates the story of the confrontation between the two brothers, Jacob and Esau. The Torah discloses the tremendous fear that gripped Jacob's heart as he journeyed to meet the brother who, years before, had vowed to kill him. Note the double expression: *Vayira Ya'akov m'eod vayeitzer lo*, 'And Jacob feared greatly and was in distress' (Genesis 32: 8).

Now, we can appreciate why Jacob entertained fear, but the double expression surely indicates far more than that. It suggests absolute terror, which surprises many of our commentators who cannot equate this with the faith and righteousness of Jacob. Surely Jacob had faith that God would protect him? Indeed, earlier, when He instructed him to leave Laban's house, and return to his own land of Canaan, God accompanied that instruction with the promise, *v'eitivah immach*, 'I shall deal well with you' (see verse 10 of our sidrah). So, armed with God's promise of protection and prosperity, why was the righteous Jacob so 'doubly afraid'?

Rashi has an interesting answer. Jacob, he says, was no more afraid than is natural even for a man of faith under those circumstances. The double expression of *vayira* and *vayeitzer*, 'he was afraid' and 'he was in distress', suggests two totally different types of fear. *Vayira* reflects the natural fear that he might, in the meantime, have fallen short of the spiritual standard expected of him, and consequently forfeited God's earlier promise of protection. The second expression, *vayeitzer*, 'and he was in distress', did not relate to his anxiety for his own life, but for

Esau's! Jacob at that moment thought about the alternative possibility, that he might kill Esau. The righteous Jacob suffered mental anguish and moral distress at being forced into a situation where he might have to perpetrate such a dreadful act.

That was the nature of Jacob. And that remains the Jewish attitude to violence and war. It is of no consequence whether or not we can justify violence as self-defence, the thought that we might be forced to shed blood is always a source of genuine distress to us. In modern times, a prime minister of Israel, Golda Meir, expressed this so accurately when she said: 'We can forgive the Arabs for killing us; but we cannot forgive them for making us kill them!'

There is a powerful message here for our younger generation to take away. It will not have escaped their notice that there has never been such a thing as an Israeli suicide bomber. There is only one recorded case, that of Baruch Goldstein, who burst into a mosque and fired indiscriminately at the worshippers. That episode is one that Israel deeply regretted. It was a blot on our moral record. Our enemies rejoice in the streets at the death of any innocent Jew. The more Jews they can kill, the greater their pleasure. For us, on the other hand, the thought of being the cause of the death of one single person, even an Esau, is too terrible to contemplate. When, in the heat of battle, an Israeli tank accidentally fires at an innocent, or even not so innocent, bystander, there is a military inquiry. When our enemies kill and maim scores of Jews by sending in a suicide bomber, there is rejoicing.

We inhabit a different moral planet. We affirm life; we view every person as having been created in the image of God. We could never think of consciously hurting others. War, for us, is a necessary evil. Jews will never fight other than in self-defence.

We are expected to cultivate and to promote a culture of sympathy, concern and charitableness. Our heightened moral conscience impels us to pursue the path of peace and understanding, and to avoid conflict at all cost. We have to be sensitive not only towards the needs and problems of our friends but also towards those of our enemies. Our desire should always be to enrich not only our own life but the lives of all men; to make the world a better place, not only for us and our families and friends, but for all mankind.

It is a tall order; but we have to make an attempt at it. And this sidrah inspires us in that direction. It holds out the ideal that we might also feel something of that same fear that gripped Jacob of ever harming others or causing them pain.

CHAPTER ELEVEN

Vayeishev:
Combining privilege
and responsibility

The story recounted in this sidrah is as fascinating as it is meaningful. It is a true commentary on human life, about how to behave and how not to behave, about how to cope with privilege and how to handle it responsibly.

Joseph began life as a shepherd boy in the sleepy, rustic country of Canaan, and ended it as a leader of the most cultured and sophisticated country of the ancient Near East. He was a dreamer; but his dreams were not idle or selfish. They were related to his burning ambition to do something with his life, to make a difference. He dreamed of becoming first a family, and then a national leader; and, from a tender age, we may speculate that he had, at the back of his mind, a firm conviction that, through his efforts, God's grand plan for the future of his family would be fulfilled. He would certainly have been told by his father, Jacob, of the promise God made to his own grandfather, Abraham, that his offspring would one day become a great nation. It is not difficult, therefore, to detect the origins of Joseph's dreams, the vision that inspired him and the passion that impelled him to develop and finely hone those powers of leadership that he detected within himself, and which even Pharaoh was later to acknowledge.

Joseph was a privileged young man in every sense. His aged father adored him, and, perhaps as recognition of his future role as leader of the Israelite clan, he presented him with a coat of many colours, a mark of rank and leadership.

But with privilege comes responsibility, and this was something that Joseph, because of his youth, was not yet able to handle. Only later did he learn the art of diplomacy, helped immeasurably by the struggle for survival when he was sold into slavery, and later when he had to use all his wits to survive and to escape the dangers of life in the Egyptian prison.

While still in his father's house he was singularly lacking in people skills. He antagonized his brothers by telling tales about them to his father, and by revealing to them the details of the dreams he had, about how they would all come bowing down before him. Joseph had no doubt about his privileged position in the family, but he was woefully lacking in the sense of responsibility and diplomacy that must go hand in hand with privilege if it is not to ignite the jealousy of the less endowed.

From the time of Bar Mitzvah onwards a Jewish male is invested with both privilege and responsibility. These are exemplified in the three high profile mitzvot that become operative from that time on. The first is the ability to be counted as part of a minyan. Although this might be construed as a privilege – in the same sense that performing any other mitzvah in the service of God is a privilege – yet it is more a token of responsibility. It is a summons to attend synagogue as often as possible, not only to pray in those ideal spiritual surroundings but also to ensure that a minyan, a public service, will be maintained. This will guarantee that religious and communal life will not be interrupted or decline, and also that those, such as mourners and those observing a yahrzeit, who require a minyan in order to recite Kaddish, will always have that facility.

Those who get out of a warm bed to be at shul at around 6.30 a.m. during the extended High Holyday Selichot period and through the festival of Succot, will concur that making up a minyan may well seem more a religious responsibility than a privilege.

And the same goes for those who cannot attend synagogue on a weekday morning, such as secondary school pupils and students who have to leave their homes very early in the morning in order to make a long journey to school or college. They must also put on their tefillin, the second mitzvah that begins at Bar Mitzvah, and

33

pray privately with as much *kavvanah*, concentration, as possible. This may also be not too easy, due to the distraction of the other members of the household, getting up, banging doors, playing their radios, barging into one's room while one is trying to concentrate on the prayers, and raising their voices. This is very much a ritual of 'responsibility', rather than privilege.

The third mitzvah that comes with Bar Mitzvah is that of being called up to the reading of the Torah. That may be construed as essentially a privilege, a personal honour. Public proclamation is made of one's Hebrew name. One walks ceremoniously to the *bimah*, and everyone responds to the blessing one makes. In a large synagogue, with hundreds of worshippers, it is a highly prized privilege, only given to those who are celebrating special events in their family life or, God forbid, to those who have just got up from sitting *shivah*, those who are observing a *yahrzeit* or who have just recovered from an illness.

So becoming Bar Mitzvah involves three special mitzvot, all of which are, *ideally*, synagogue based: putting on one's tefillin each day, praying with a *minyan*, and hearing or being called to the reading of the Torah. The first two involve discipline and responsibility; the third involves privilege.

Jewish character training involves synthesizing them to the extent that every responsibility that one is called upon by the community to shoulder is viewed as a privilege. Conversely, that every privilege, recognition or honour that the community might confer upon one should ever be viewed as a responsibility and a call to undertake extra and more ambitious acts of communal service.

CHAPTER TWELVE

Mikeitz:
On being 'one of God's miracles'

At the beginning of the saga of Joseph's life he is described as *na'ar*, a mere lad, someone lacking in tact and sensitivity. And that is what got him into such trouble in his relationship with his other brothers. He *sensed* he was chosen for greatness, but he lacked the *sense* required to attain it. He only developed and matured after he had confronted adversity and was thrown onto his own resources. As long as he thought he could rely on other people, his suffering was prolonged. And this is how the Midrash explains the opening words of the sidrah: *Vayehi mikeitz sh'natayim yamim*, 'And it came to pass at the end of two years [in prison]' (Genesis 41: 1). We recall that, in prison, he had asked the royal cupbearer, whose dream he had successfully interpreted, to do him a favour and to keep him in mind and mention his plight to Pharaoh (Genesis 40: 15).

This may seem to us a fairly reasonable and harmless request. However, the Midrash (*Ber. Rabb.* 89: 3) does not think so. It maintains that on account of Joseph's having placed all his trust and reliance on another, and having asked of him two favours – to 'remember' him and to 'mention' him to Pharaoh, two further years were added by God to the time Joseph spent in prison. Hence *Vayehi mikeitz sh'natayim yamim*, 'And it came to pass after two years' (Genesis 41: 1).

But was that not a rather heavy price to pay for such a natural request for help? By way of explanation, the Midrash quotes the Psalmist, 'Happy is the man who makes the Lord his trust and does not turn to the arrogant' (Psalm 40: 5). This is elucidated by the eighteenth-century commentator, the *Netziv* of Volozhin (Rabbi Naftali Zvi Yehudah Berlin), in his *Ha'amek Davar*. This is intended to show, he says, that in a crisis one should rely neither on human beings alone nor on God alone to provide a miracle. Of course, those who seek a way out of difficult situations should not fail to pray for divine aid, for frequently God answers by sending earthly agents to work on His behalf. But if one tries to manage without God entirely, and put one's trust exclusively in human beings, they often prove to be broken reeds, unreliable, unsympathetic and unhelpful.

The point is beautifully illustrated in a story told of David Ben-Gurion and Chief Rabbi Isaac Herzog. In the tense days of the 1948 Israeli War of Independence, it is said that Ben-Gurion came to the rabbi and asked why God does not send the Israelis some miracles to get them out of their present crisis? Rav Herzog replied, 'But Prime Minister, He has: You are one of God's miracles!'

Indeed, one of the reasons the sages lay such inordinate stress on the miracle of the Chanukah oil, rather than on the military prowess of the Maccabees, was precisely so that we should appreciate the element of the miraculous – by which they meant the hand of God – in absolutely everything that happens in life. What we perceive as our own achievements, be they military, medical, scientific or cultural, have their origins in a divine creativity that has been shared with man. We are all 'one of God's miracles'.

At certain times of our lives we sense it particularly powerfully. A baby is born, and the grateful, doting parents look at it and have that overwhelming feeling that birth in general, and their baby in particular, is truly 'one of God's miracles'. The same applies if we are delivered from danger, or recover from serious illness, against all odds. Indeed, we thank God three times a day, in the *Modim* prayer for *al nisecha sheb'chol yom immanu*, 'the miracles that we experience *every day*'. The challenge of life is that, once having been born a divine miracle, we have to endeavour, throughout our lives, to live in gratitude for it and to be worthy of it.

There are truly many occasions and situations, in the lives of us all, when the privilege is offered to us of touching the lives of others, of making a difference, of offering help, advice, love and support, as representatives of the Almighty Himself. And when we transform the lives of God's children in such a way, then, for that person, our unexpected relief and intervention truly makes us 'one of God's miracles'.

Youth is the point of transition from childhood to adulthood. We can live the life of the young Joseph, as an immature *na'ar*, until our dying day, or we can be 'one of God's miracles'. We can remain a child, expecting and demanding that our every need will be attended to by others, or we can grow up and realize that life is not like that, and that we have to make the most of our strengths and resources. When problems, or, God forbid, adversity, comes we can either drown in it or we can use it as a springboard to a more mature, focused and independent approach to life. The choice is ours. There is no reason why the miracle we commemorate on Chanukah, for example, should not last throughout the year, and every year of our life. And we should never forget that the miracle was only the climax of three years of struggle and war. Life is a multi-textured fabric, and we must take the smooth with the rough.

CHAPTER THIRTEEN

Vayigash:
Converting adversity
into advantage

Over the past few decades, a substantial number of young South African Jewish families – not all of them dentists! – have made aliyah to this country, and have enriched our synagogue and community life immeasurably, bringing with them new vitality and new ideas. Had life and politics in that country remained on an even keel, with the white man still exercising his traditional imperialist role in Africa, it is very doubtful whether those families would have left that country, with its beauty, opportunity and comforts, sunshine and open spaces.

But that did not happen. Instead, a total political upheaval took place, and a bitter struggle on the part of the black population of that country for equality and independence, led by courageous visionaries like Nelson Mandela and Desmond Tutu, men who were prepared to suffer up to twenty years' imprisonment for their ideals.

Inevitably, many young Jewish South African families felt uncomfortable, morally and physically, in that climate of uncertainty, upheaval and reverse discrimination against whites, and they decided to move to Great Britain and other countries. Rightly or wrongly, they perceived British society as safer and more settled and that the country was a more welcoming place for Jews.

The message of their presence in Great Britain is a powerful one, and may be summed up by the maxim, 'every cloud has a silver lining'. In other words: a bleak situation, namely the decline of a once great, large and prosperous Jewish community, has resulted, through the voluntary exile of its talented young people, in the unexpected strengthening and revitalization of our community here in Britain.

I believe that there is also a profound religious message here, on the issue of faith. Very often people facing serious personal, family or business problems give in to despair. They see their lives in turmoil, sometimes having to give up their jobs, sever their relationships, and surrender their physical and emotional comforts. They believe at that point that they will never survive that crisis. Their optimism and faith simply evaporates.

So often, had they the capacity to glimpse into the future, they simply would not have believed the good fortune they would see mapped out. Most would soon come to realize that change and adjustment are not necessarily negative experiences. Often they are the natural vehicles to the destination of advancement, greater peace of mind and opportunity, and better fortune. If we have the right state of mind, if we have faith in God and in ourselves, if we work hard and have a vision, then we can convert adversity, even exile, into a blessing.

And perhaps that is another reason why the family of Jacob had to go into exile in Egypt before being restored to the land of Canaan. Namely, to learn the lesson of never becoming complacent, never taking their prosperity for granted, never remaining comfortable as mere herdsmen of their family's flocks in Canaan. They were destined for something much greater than that, namely to become a great nation, the Chosen People, the recipients of God's law.

But first they had to learn to cope with the challenge of change, how to muster the courage of sustaining faith when all around had abandoned it, and when so many of life's tragedies seemed to render it an illusion. First they had to learn how to convert adversity into advantage, because that was an essential quality for any emerging nation, especially for a nation of spiritual pioneers.

So many young people from South Africa took a giant leap of faith when they left their parents, family, friends and homeland to put down fresh roots on far-off shores, as do a growing number of young Jewish men and women around the world when they make *aliyah* to Israel. Our nation of 'wandering Jews' has survived and flourished only because we imbibed and nurtured that faith. And it has never let us down.

CHAPTER FOURTEEN

Vayigash:
On being comfortable
with oneself

When the brothers of Joseph were presented to Pharaoh and he asked them about their profession, they answered, *ro'ei tzo'n avadecha*, 'your servants are shepherds' (Genesis 47: 3). By that they meant that they looked after and fed the sheep in the fields. Significantly, that was not the answer that Joseph had primed them beforehand to give. He had told them to say, *anshei mikneh hayyu avadecha*, 'your servants are owners of herds of cattle' (Genesis 46: 33–34). Why did they depart from their script?

It has been suggested that Joseph wanted to boost the status of his brothers in the eyes of Pharaoh. He did not want them to present themselves as mere shepherds, the lowest rung on the social and economic ladder, people generally without education, particular skills or business capability. He wanted them to be regarded as an asset to Egypt, people of wealth, status and talent who could benefit the country. Hence he told them to say that they were *anshei mikneh*, ranchers, *owners* of herds. The brothers, on the other hand, were simple folk who did not put much score by wealth and status. They knew that possessions were not a measure of a person, but rather what he or she does with their wealth. They were not out to impress, neither were they impressed by the opulence of Pharaoh's palace. And hence they had no qualms about telling Pharaoh that they were simple shepherds.

This is an admirable philosophy as we enter adult life. The message is that one should just be oneself. Other considerations apart, people are generally quite astute, and they easily see through an act or pretence. Those who try to pass themselves off as cleverer, wealthier, more educated or talented than they really are, are very soon unmasked. We can only fool some of the people some of the time!

We should realize that we are all endowed with some special quality – of personality, of manner, of looks, of nature – that is unique to us. And those appealing attributes have nothing to do with money, education or talent. They are our 'natural' characteristics; they define the inner person. And it is generally those attributes that make us attractive to others.

The message is: Be natural. That is what the brothers of Joseph were. They did not want to put on a show for other people, even for Pharaoh. They wanted to be comfortable with themselves. It is a timely message for our modern society that is so obsessed with image. We should rather isolate the good qualities we know we possess – those that come naturally to us – and cultivate them. They will be enough to impress the people we really need to impress. They will realize quite readily that they are getting the real thing, the real 'you', and no pretence will ever be required. You will be comfortable with them. They will be comfortable with you. And, above all, you will be comfortable with yourself!

CHAPTER FIFTEEN

Vayechi:
How we earn blessings

With this sidrah we conclude the reading of the first book of the Torah, the book of Bereishit, an account of the childhood and adolescence of our nation and its growing maturity as a budding nation. The parallel with young adulthood and the transition from the childhood phase to that of becoming fully-fledged members of the Jewish people, with all the agonies and ecstasies that that involves, is inescapable.

The sidrah Vayechi, means, 'And he lived' – and it may be read as a commentary on the way life should be lived: fully and constructively, not selfishly or vainly. That message is reflected in Jacob's last words to his children. On his death bed he addressed each of them in turn, referring to their unique character traits, strengths and weaknesses, deserved status, as well as the things each one could be proud of and the situations (as in the case of Shimon and Levi) wherein they behaved less than honourably, bringing shame upon their father and family.

The blessings end with the Torah stating something very curious: *Vayevarech otam, ish asher kevirkato beirach otam*, 'And he blessed them, each man *according to his blessing* he blessed them' (Genesis 49: 28). There is such a repetition of 'blessing' here that it is far from clear what the text is actually saying. If it means, as generally understood, that Jacob gave each of his children his own separate and unique blessing, then it should have stated, simply, *Vayevarcheim, ish kevirchato*, 'And he blessed them, each of them with his own blessing'.

It seems, however, that this complicated phraseology was intended to tell us something more than that Jacob gave a blessing, even a unique blessing, to each son. It seems to be implying that Jacob's blessing to each one was that he should achieve the blessing that was inherent within him ('each man according to his own blessing'). He blessed them that they should each achieve their full potential, build on their innate spirituality, and cultivate their inherent qualities.

The message is simple: *We are the source of our own blessings.* If we want blessing in life, we have to create and nurture it. God already told Abraham, 'I will bless those that bless you, and those that curse you I will curse'. In other words, we ourselves can determine to a large extent the quality of our lives. If we want fulfilment, we have to lead fulfilling, constructive lives. If we want to feel blessed we have to bless others, by extending to them good cheer, sympathy, generosity and friendship. Just like the miracle of Chanukah, wherein there was already enough oil for one day, and the miracle extended the potential inherent in that oil, so it is with blessing. If we create a measure of blessing, and dispense it to those around us, God will enhance and augment it, and direct it inwards, so that we become not only its dispensers but also its recipients.

Now we may understand the meaning of Jacob having blessed each of his sons 'according to his blessing' – his own, *self-generated* blessing. For those embarking on their adult life, there is a profound challenge contained in this message.

CHAPTER SIXTEEN

Vayechi:
The strength to become a man

The very opening verse of today's haftarah contains a succinct message. King David senses that his life is coming to an end, and he summons his beloved son, Solomon, to give him his final blessing and to leave him with some guidance and final instructions.

He begins by telling Solomon, 'I am going the way of all the earth' — *Vechazakta vehayita l'ish* — 'Now you be strong and show yourself a man' (1 Kings 2: 2). In today's dangerous world, where moral standards and respect for others seem largely to have disappeared, one truly needs 'to be strong' if one wants to attain to manhood — *vehayita l'ish* — with one's moral and religious values intact.

Support for this was provided by Home Office statistics suggesting that some 220,000 young people between the age of 11 to 18 would be considering taking cocaine, heroin and ecstasy over the new year period, with most of them hopelessly unaware of their potentially disastrous consequences. The government was initiating a campaign, therefore, to dissuade them from indulging (see *Crime and Justice Survey 2003*, Home Office Research, Development and Statistics Directorate).

How tragic it is that those young people, who could be filling their leisure time constructively, and living their lives with dignity and honour, choose instead to escape from reality and undermine their own and society's self-respect. Their *Vayechi*, their 'life' and our Jewishly committed youth's *Vayechi*, are truly poles apart.

But we cannot be smug. And it is very easy to get enticed – by so-called friends at school, at university or in the workplace – into degrading activities. And even young people from the best families, if they do not exercise great self-control and vigilance, can become victims. This is precisely why King David told his son Solomon, *Vechazakta, vehayita l'ish*, 'Be strong and show yourself a man'. It takes strength – of character and will – to become 'a man', morally mature, as defined by our exacting religious standards.

Significantly, we conclude the reading of the sidrah Vayyechi with the rousing congregational shout, *Chazak chazak v'nitchazeik*, 'Be strong, be strong, and let us strengthen ourselves'. That should be the slogan of our youth community: A call to each and every member to enrich Jewish 'life' through the strength – spiritual and moral – that they all have to muster and share with each other.

PART TWO
SHEMOT

CHAPTER SEVENTEEN

Shemot:
Countering old and new
propaganda

There is one aspect of the account of the enslavement of the
Israelites, as recorded in this sidrah, which constitutes a most
chilling parallel to our modern situation where Arab propaganda
presents Israel in the worst possible light, casting her in the role of
a heartless aggressor. In the 2006 Israeli retaliation against the murderous Hizbollah terrorists in Lebanon, the latter's propaganda
machine even applied the term 'Nazis' to Israel for the killing of
innocent Lebanese civilians. The fact that Israel had no alternative
but to attack the terrorist's rocket-launching pads that had been
established next to blocks of flats, schools and hospitals in the
heart of Lebanese cities was not considered, even by the majority
of western media correspondents. Neither did they linger, in their
television reports, over the horrific images of killed, maimed and
homeless Israelis, to the same extent that they did over the
Lebanese casualties. Israel's enemies were pleased to exploit the
latter carnage, against the backcloth of which they were able to
justify and glorify those murderous and deranged suicide
bombers who for so long had taken such a terrible toll of innocent Israeli lives.

Pharaoh had already shown how easy it was to manipulate the
masses by feeding them with slanted propaganda, and thereby dis-
torting reality in a way that injected irrational fear and loathing of
the Israelites into the hearts of the native Egyptians.

Hear what the Torah reports:

> *Vayomer el ammo*, And Pharaoh said to his people – *Hinnei 'am b'nei Yisrael rav v'atzum mimmenu* – Behold the Israelites are more numerous and stronger than us. Come and let us deal astutely in relation to them – *pen yirbeh* – lest they multiply, and if we are embroiled in any war, they will make an alliance with our enemy, and wage war with us and drive us from the land. (Exodus 1: 10)

We have represented here all the hallmarks of false propaganda. First, the fact that the great and mighty Pharaoh, who had at his command the finest army, comprising tens of thousands of troops, armed to the teeth and with countless chariots, yet, quite preposterously, presenting as a threat to the security of the state the peace-loving Israelites of Goshen, people with no history of warfare behind them, and absolutely no military experience or equipment. It was true that their families were rapidly increasing, but family life was clearly their priority, not military action of any kind.

The Israelites did not even have a single representative in government or wider administration. They had made no inroads into the corridors of influence and power in Egypt. It is doubtful that they even spoke the Egyptian language! (The choice of Moses as leader, with the mission to go to Pharaoh and secure the release of the Israelites, was that, in addition to his own qualities, he was probably the only Hebrew who spoke fluent Egyptian, having been reared in Pharaoh's palace.)

But Pharaoh did not wish to be distracted by the truth. He told his people that the Israelites were *rav v'atzum mimmenu*, 'more numerous *and stronger* than us'. Already highly suspicious of those strange Hebrew outsiders, who looked different, who kept to themselves, living in a separate part of the country and practising their own ancestral traditions and faith, the Egyptians were only too ready – like other societies after them down the ages – to swallow the big lie, based on their irrational fear of the stranger. We call that 'xenophobia'. It is a big word, with an even bigger following.

Note a further, most revealing, inconsistency in the argument

Pharaoh uses to rouse the Egyptian rabble against the Hebrews. First he says that they are 'more numerous than us', and then he says 'Come and let us deal astutely with them, *pen yirbeh, lest* they multiply'. We can see clearly how Pharaoh was fabricating the situation and contradicting himself in order to implant fear and hatred of the Israelites into the hearts of his people.

And this ploy has been used from the days of Pharaoh until the present in the cause of anti-Semitism. Pharaoh had a means of brainwashing his people. He could address them, send round proclamations and disinformation. The Israelites, on the other hand, had no media with which to counter and expose those false allegations.

And to this day people have been exploiting that same xenophobia, especially against Israel and the Jewish people, rewriting history, falsifying evidence, perpetrating terror and blaming the innocent victims. And that is why we keep reading and rereading, year in, year out, the age-old stories from our Torah, of how we were the objects of poisonous propaganda, as a means of depriving us of our rights, our freedom, our destiny and, ultimately, our lives.

Moses' efforts to rebut Pharaoh's false propaganda, and to present his people's case in the most appealing and persuasive way possible contains a special message for our youth: to study the history of our people, especially its modern history, so that they may become fully informed and able to offer themselves as courageous defenders of, and impressive spokesmen for, our people and its cause, whether at school, university or the workplace.

CHAPTER EIGHTEEN

Va'eira:
The challenge of
Jewish leadership

The early sidrot of the Book of Shemot provide a snapshot of the leadership qualities of Moses. So many leaders throughout history have used their positions as an ego-trip, to wield power over, and even to enslave, others, or as a passport to a life of wealth and luxury. Moses served as a unique kind of leader who cared nothing for his own comforts and who devoted his entire life to bringing Israel close to God.

That Moses did not exploit his position for any personal gain may be shown from his response to the personal attack on him levelled by Korach and his cohort of rebels who accused Moses of tyranny and having abused his position of leadership. Moses was able to say categorically to God, who certainly knew the truth of every situation, 'I have never taken so much as a donkey from any of them, nor have I harmed a single one of them' (Numbers 16: 15).

History abounds with examples of tribal and other leaders who were so fiercely committed to the notion of the superiority of their own race or tribe that, on assuming power, they unleash terrible suffering on the minority peoples or religions that lived among them. Again Moses serves as a unique example of a leader who not only took his own people out of Egypt, but also permitted the *eirev rav*, a mixed multitude of peoples enslaved by the Egyptians, to share Israel's destiny and to leave Egypt with them (Exodus 12: 38).

That is what being a Jew means: caring for all those who are happy to share our destiny. It is very tragic that the Palestinians have, until now, put themselves on a violent collision course with our people, because our mission is to live in peace and brotherhood with our neighbours, certainly not to kill and maim them. And we look forward to the day when we can repeat the circumstances of our first Exodus to the Promised Land and offer our freedom and the fruits of our progress to the neighbours around us.

But leadership is not confined to countries and peoples. We are all given the mitzvah, the mission and the challenge, to serve and to lead, in our own local communities and synagogues, and to play our part in making them as successful and vibrant as possible. Like Moses, we do it exclusively for the communal benefit, and never for our own personal advantage.

CHAPTER NINETEEN

Bo:
Tefillin and our
'work-driven' week

In the last (*Shevii*) section of our sidrah there are two paragraphs (Exodus 13: 1–10; 11–16) which are prescribed for inclusion inside the tefillin. The usual reason given as to why we only wear tefillin on working days, not on Sabbaths and festivals, is that tefillin are described in the *Shema* by the word *ot*, 'a sign', an outward demonstration of Israel's sacred covenant with God, as it says: *Vehayah l'ot al yadcha*, 'And they shall be for a sign upon your hand' (Exodus 13: 9, 16).

This sign of the tefillin is necessary on weekdays, in order to consecrate one's workaday life, to remember God and to inject a little sanctity into a working day that, in so many cases, is characterized by activity that is quite remote from sacred and ethical considerations. On Shabbat and festivals, however, this should not be necessary since those days of rest, prayer and celebration are powerful enough 'signs of consecration' without the extra sign of the tefillin.

But we may suggest another explanation of the inapplicability of wearing tefillin on those days, in the light of the workaholic culture that is the hallmark of western countries. Tefillin are so obviously the symbol of a work-driven day; and in the way they are worn they caution us against the excesses of work obsession. We bind them around our arms and head, as if to demonstrate how restrained we feel by the myriad demands of our workplace. The straps that we wind around us symbolize how slave-like we can become. They remind us of chains, preventing us from escaping from our manifold tasks and deadlines.

Each morning the tefillin serve as a mirror to our lives, crying out to us,

> Do not become working animals. Remember that you have only one ultimate Master to serve. No one else has the right to claim sovereignty over your life. Take some time off in the day to find yourself in prayer; to rediscover your individuality as a being created in God's image, worthy of entering into dialogue with the Creator of the universe. Let no one imagine, therefore, that they can rob you of your freedom to interact with your parents, your spouse, your children, your friends and, above all, your Maker. Allow no one to convert you into a robot, a profit-producing machine.

So the tefillin, which symbolize and caution against work obsession, are so obviously inappropriate to the Shabbat or *yom tov*, when we do consecrate time and celebrate our physical and mental liberation, when we do, indeed, take our rest and turn our back on all the constraints and appointments that imprison us during the other days of the week, and when we do jump off the treadmill of business, ambition and competition.

In the unusual context of Cain and Abel, the Torah's use of the word *sha'ah*, which, in later Hebrew, came to mean, 'a period of time, an hour', demonstrates most forcefully Judaism's concept of time. Both brothers offered sacrifices to God, but *V'el kayin v'el minchato lo sha'ah*, 'to Cain and his sacrifice God did not *sha'ah*', literally, 'give the time of day', or regard as of any consequence (Genesis 4: 5).

Thus, in Judaism, 'time', *sha'ah*, equates to that which is of real *consequence*, that which is of primary significance. Time is the medium through which we can make ourselves, and the offerings of our hands, pleasing to God. Cain's 'time' was not devoted to God; so God did not reciprocate, and give him 'time' or recognition. When, on the other hand, we do make time for a worthy enterprise – attending synagogue, learning, lending an ear to someone with a problem or visiting someone in hospital or, God forbid, sitting *shivah* – then we truly are consecrating time. Then we truly are using it for the purpose for which it was created.

The common belief is that when we are not at work we are at play. Judaism believes that when we are not at work, and are thus able to take control of our own time, that is when true responsibility is called for. The most accurate monitor of a person's quality of heart and religious inclination lies in the way he utilizes his or her spare time.

Any hospital chaplain will confirm that no dying patient ever expressed regret that he had not spent more time in the office. The regret is, invariably, that he or she did not have a closer relationship, or spend more time, with their family, that they had lived a selfish life, had begrudged allocating time to worthy activities and causes, had been a slave to timetables imposed by others and to valueless routines and selfish indulgences. In short, that they had squandered their God-given time.

The message from this sidrah and from the tefillin is so vital for young adults just learning the art of managing their spare time. It calls to them to be the masters of their time, to use it wisely and religiously, and not to let it master them. It challenges them to *make* time for causes that matter and for people that need a little of that time. So that, unlike the case of Cain, God will find plenty of time for them, will highly regard them, and bless them with all that is good.

CHAPTER TWENTY

Beshalach:
Messages from the manna

Every young person is taught that we have two challot on Shabbat because on that day the Israelites in the desert were not allowed to go out and collect the manna, the food that fell around the outskirts of the camp. This was because it was forbidden to travel outside the limits of an inhabited area on that holy day that is reserved for tranquillity and relaxation, not for the undertaking of travel. So God sent a double portion on Fridays, so that they might cook and bake enough food to last them also for Shabbat.

The Torah tells us that there were some greedy people, however, who, having disregarded Moses' instruction and having taken their double portion on the Friday, also went out searching for manna in the fields on Shabbat morning (Exodus 16: 27). Needless to say, they found no manna.

We learn from this three lessons: First, the importance of proper Shabbat observance, and of buying, cooking and preparing all our food in advance. This enables us – and especially the women, for whom, otherwise, Shabbat would be the same as every other day of the week – to celebrate it as a day of rest, prayer, study and family celebration.

Secondly, it teaches us not to be greedy, but always to be content and satisfied with the blessings that we are sent. Moderation in eating, drinking and, indeed, in every other physical pleasure, is taught by the fact that God determined that everyone should have exactly the same measured amount, an *Omer*, of manna to eat. Indeed, those who had gathered in from the field more than that prescribed amount discovered that by the time they got it back to their tent it had miraculously reduced to the prescribed allocation! Similarly, those who could only carry a smaller amount found, on arriving back home, that it had expanded to an Omer's size! (Exodus 16: 17; see Rashi ad loc).

Thirdly, it teaches us to have faith, and to rely on God's promises, rather than to think that we are masters of our own fate, and that we alone determine what our own future will bring and what will be the extent of our prosperity. If we deserve it, God will protect us, send us happiness and contentment, and — like the double portion of manna — provide in abundance for all our needs.

CHAPTER TWENTY-ONE

Beshalach:
Women's religious equality

In the sidrah Beshalach we find Miriam leading the women out in a victory celebration of song and dance for their deliverance at the Red Sea. R. Kalonymos Kalman Epstein, author of *Ma'or Va-Shemesh*, views the dance of the women, and the lyrical formula of the song they sang – almost, but not exactly, identical to that sung by Moses – as reflecting women's loftier level of spiritual perception.

When Moses initiated the *Shirat Ha-yam*, the Song of the Red Sea, and led the men in its recitation, he did not employ dancing. The men merely sang; and according to tradition it was a responsive song, led by Moses. It was also a poetically structured composition, and therefore subject to the literary style that governs biblical poetry. That contrived structuring is reflected in the way the Song is set out in the Torah (and in our chumashim). It is represented in the shape of the bricks of a wall, with one brick bridging the join of the two bricks on the line below. The men were, symbolically, wall-like; they were rather rigid, stiff, self-conscious.

When Miriam led the women in celebration, on the other hand, they all instinctively joined hands and created a circle for dancing. It was not merely the voice that offered praise; it was the entire body in a symbolic demonstration of total oneness with God. Their arms, legs and entire body were involved in that uninhibited outpouring of ecstatic spiritual joy and rhythmic movement. Perhaps this underlies the phrase *Vateitzena kol ha-nashim*, 'And all the women came out', an emphasis that does not occur with reference to the men. It does not say *Az yashir Mosheh v'chol b'nei Yisrael*, 'Then Moses and all the Israelites sang'. The men *sang* praise; the women *embodied* it. They actually became the very personification of praise of God.

Rav Kalonymos views the women's circle as a mystical expression of equality. In a circle, all points on the circumference are equidistant from the centre point. The centre point is God, at the epicentre of His universe. In the world we inhabit there are hierarchies, there are tensions and competitiveness between the sexes, and between the members of each sex. Men dominate and attempt to impose a passive role upon women, especially in matters of spirituality.

But that is not the plan for the future, for the Messianic order. At that time all will receive God's light in equal measure, and spiritual inequalities will all vanish. And this equality, for Rav Kalonymos, is symbolized in the circle that Miriam initiates for the women and the dance that expresses the totality of their spiritual exuberance.

That same idea is reflected in our Haftarah, where the judge and prophetess Devorah becomes indispensable to both the physical and the spiritual security of the nation. The Israelite general, Barak ben Avinoam, approaches her and craves her presence at the battle against the Canaanites, in order to guarantee the Israelites victory. She agrees, but tells him that, as a result, the glory will ultimately be hers, as people will credit the victory to her spiritual influence (Judges 4: 9).

The Haftarah thus complements the mystical interpretation Rav Kalonymos gave to the differences between the ways Moses and Miriam sang their praises, and it reflects a future situation when women are regarded as indispensable to the physical and the spiritual protection of Israel.

At the present time, with many women immersing themselves in Torah study at seminaries and occupying academic posts in Jewish Studies, that ideal of spiritual equality is well on the way to being realized. Indeed, it is no accident that most words for wisdom, learning and religious practice are feminine: *Torah, chochmah, binah, da'at, tevunah, eitzah, toshi'ah, mitzvah, halachah, mishnah* and *Gemarah*. With women serving as equals of the men in the Israeli army, as well as in the security organizations of Jewish communities around the world, their equal role in the physical protection of our people cannot be denied.

The challenge of our young women is to join that growing band of their peers who are taking their place as leaders within the religious community, and to avail themselves of all the facilities that now exist for women to study and train in order to realize their full spiritual potential, and to make a worthy contribution to the study of our Torah and the intensification and enrichment of religious life.

CHAPTER TWENTY-TWO

Yitro:
Rushing in where others
feared to tread

When Moses first approached the Israelites about accepting the Torah, their response was almost too good to be true. *Vaya'anu kol ha'am yachdav*, 'And all the people responded instantaneously', *Kol asher dibber Hashem na'aseh*, 'Whatever God says we will obey' (Exodus 19: 8). The Talmud records a comment by one critic of Israel that our people were quite rash in agreeing to accept everything in the Torah before they had even heard what it demanded of them. After all, what sane person enters into a contract before he has had time to read and digest the text fully and to know exactly what commitment he is accepting? Was it not a valid criticism of our people, then? Indeed, when we consider how Israel began to disobey so many of its laws no sooner had they received the Torah, does not that criticism seem completely irrefutable?

Now the Midrash has a famous comment on that verse, 'Whatever God says we will obey'. It depicts God, before he gave the Torah to Israel, as offering it to the other main peoples of the East. First he went to the offspring of Esau. 'What is written in the Torah?', they wisely asked God. 'Thou shalt not kill', replied God. 'Thou shalt not kill? Impossible. Killing is our way-of-life. Thank you; but no thank you, God!'

God then went to the Ammonites and offered it to them. They also demanded to know what this Torah required of them. 'Thou shalt not commit adultery', answered God. The Ammonites smirked. 'No, that's not for us!' God then went to the Ishmaelites

62

and offered the Torah to them. On being told that it contained the regulation, 'Thou shalt not steal', they replied, 'Good try, God. We appreciate the offer, but we don't think it quite suits our profile!' So, after hawking the Torah around all the other tribes, God came and offered it to Israel who grabbed it with both hands, shouting, 'Whatever God says we will obey' (Sifre on Vezot Haberachah; see also Rashi on Deuteronomy 33: 2).

But that Midrash is problematic. For surely the all-knowing God knew before He went to those other nations that they would refuse it, and that He would ultimately have to come to Israel who would enthusiastically receive it! Why, then, did He bother in the first place to offer it to those whom He knew would snub Him? Why did He not give Israel the honour of going to them at the very outset? Would that not have been a just reward for Israel's loyalty and enthusiasm? Would it not also have avoided the rebuffs that God had to suffer at the hands of those other nations?

Our answer is a simple one, yet it contains an important message for a young adult. It is that it was precisely because God *does* foresee the future that he was unhappy with Israel's response and did not go to her first. God must have been singularly unimpressed when He looked into the future and saw Israel say, 'We do not need to know what it contains, we will obey it all!' For that is an immature response. Indeed such a level of faith is beyond the attainment of any human, let alone an entire nation.

One cannot totally and enthusiastically accept and observe every detail of a contract if one has not read and studied its contents. It would be foolhardy. For one thing, one cannot be sure that one has the ability or knowledge required to fulfil it. And that is precisely why ongoing Jewish education to an advanced level is so vital in order to become a fully-practising Jew. Hence the statement: Ein bur yerei cheit, 'An uneducated man cannot be God-fearing' (Ethics of the Fathers 2: 6).

While the other nations laughed at God when He revealed to them what His Torah expected of them, it was God's turn to have the last laugh when He heard Israel's exaggerated response: 'Whatever is in the Torah we will fully obey'. And for that reason, to save Israel's blushes for as long as possible, God did not offer his Torah to her immediately until He had approached, and been rebuffed by, all the other nations. In the meantime Israel would have had time to discover from Moses the broad outline of what that Torah that was being hawked around contained, and also to glean some information about it from those other surrounding nations. Hence Israel had a ready answer to those who mocked her for rashly accepting a Torah that she knew nothing about.

Two messages emerge from that Midrash. First, that study must precede observance, and that we should not think that we can perform mitzvot and leave learning about them for some future time in our lives when we are much older. Secondly, that it is rash to imagine that we can keep the entire Torah. Our ancestors could not do it, and neither can we.

If we are realistic, then, we will appreciate that Bar or Bat Mitzvah is not the period when Judaism expects a young person to master and observe the entirety of Jewish law. That would be totally unreasonable and unattainable. The Torah was given on a mountain. It takes time to climb a mountain.

Bar and Bat Mitzvah is rather the moment when the young person is expected to accept upon him or herself the challenge of studying the Torah and trying to observe as many of Judaism's mitzvot as possible. But young people have to go at a pace that is manageable and they have to set themselves targets that are realizable. At any time along the way they can accelerate the pace and intensify their observance. It will take much time, effort, learning and sacrifice to be in a position to respond as readily and unreservedly as did our ancestors at Sinai, 'Whatever God says we will obey'.

CHAPTER TWENTY-THREE

Mishpatim:
How not to make a slave
of oneself

In the sidrah Mishpatim the Torah reveals its concept of human freedom. Rather than produce a dry philosophical essay on the subject, as many modern philosophers have done, the Torah uses the model of the slave, or, more accurately, the *eved*. For, when we consider what respect and consideration the ancient Israelites had to show to the *eved* – surely the least important rank in society – and how a single assault on him could force the employer to forfeit his services, we will easily be able to deduce from there just what regard and concern we are expected to have for our neighbours over whose lives and services we have no such authority.

Significantly, the Torah has no special word for a Hebrew slave. The word *eved* comes from the verb *avad*, which has the basic and simple meaning of 'to work'. When applied to a brother who had fallen on hard times and who had therefore to sell his services to a fellow Israelite, it was meant to have no overtone of imprisonment, confinement, lowliness and deprivation of rights, such as flow from the English words, 'slave', 'slavery', and 'servile'. Indeed, the identical verb, *avad*, is used to describe our religious ritual and service of God, as in the noun *avodah*, usually translated, 'service'. And that same word is used by God as a special compliment to Abraham – *avdiy* – in order to highlight the one whose 'service' of God was so loyal and wholehearted (see Genesis 26: 24).

So if this is how the Torah insists we treat those whose services we own, imagine how we must view those who are certainly our equal in society. We must never ill-treat or discriminate against any other person whatever his social standing, the colour of his skin, his religion or his nationality. This was reinforced by the prophet Amos who told Israel – *Hallo kivnei Kushiim attem liy*, 'You are no different to the Ethiopians to Me' (Amos 9: 7). They are also My children. Both you, Israel, and I, have a duty of care toward them.

Unlike the ancient Romans, who, in the main, regarded their slaves as subhuman, transporting them in leaky, cramped vessels to slave markets across the seas, we Jews have always shown the greatest consideration to those over whose lives we have exercised a measure of control. Not surprisingly, the Talmud states, 'He who acquires a Hebrew *eved*, acquires a master for himself!' (Kiddushin 20a) And this has also influenced our treatment of those people we merely employ in our businesses. We should not only pay them their wages, but also pay them compliments; encouraging them when they have done well, showing concern and support when they or their family are ill, and rewarding them materially when profits allow.

There is an important message here for any young person. As they proceed through their teenage and student years, and start on the career ladder, they frequently discover that so many areas of life are highly competitive, that life can be a rat race, a narrow corridor through which only a handful of people can squeeze into the inner chamber of success, achievement and wealth. Many are tempted, therefore, in the process of securing their own success, to 'dumb down' a colleague, to slight his or her achievements in order to enhance their own, to be unfairly critical of their skills, or even of their looks, dress or manner. Many are truly jealous of the better opportunities that they imagine the other to have had.

If one adopts such a negative and destructive mode, one makes a slave of oneself, surrendering one's freedom to get on with one's own life and being constantly chained to considering the situation of others, while measuring one's own results by comparison with theirs. People in such a mode will never be truly free to live by their own standards, to maximize on the particular talents, strengths and abilities with which they have personally been endowed.

Today's *OK!* and *Hello!* culture sadly cultivates that attitude among young people, by glamorizing the lives and habits of those in the public eye and making envious a whole generation of those who cannot aspire to the exaggerated lifestyles that the 'stars' can afford to lead. Too many people will spend their time idly dreaming of the unattainable instead of getting on earnestly with what is certainly attainable.

The message of the sidrah *Mishpatim* is twofold: to treat everyone with respect and consideration, and not to make a slave of ourselves by ogling after the successes of others, but to be grateful for the blessings and talents with which we are endowed, and to build upon those foundations.

CHAPTER TWENTY-FOUR

Terumah:
Lessons from the Mishkan

There is a lesson to be derived from consideration of the structure of the Mishkan, the desert Sanctuary, and the reaction of our ancestors when it was completed and raised for the first time.

If the truth be told, the Israelites must have blushed. They had just come out of Egypt, with its colossal statues and structures in honour of the Pharaohs, its magnificent rock-cut temples, at such places as Luxor, Thebes and Karnak, even the ruins of which still fill visitors with awe and admiration, as well as its lofty granite pyramids and Sphinx.

And what did they see when they gazed at their new Mishkan? Well, had they lived today they would have been making comparisons with do-it-yourself (DIY) flat-packs, of poles, acacia wood boards, tent-pegs and ram-skin screens stretched around the boards. The whole structure measured a mere 100 cubits by 50, which is about 150 feet x 75 feet – the equivalent of just one and-a-quarter tennis courts! What a comparison with the vast, imposing Egyptian temples, with their entrance ramps, forecourts, gates, colonnaded inner courts, storage rooms, upward tapering towers, windowed halls and ceremonial walkways!

What lessons do we imagine the Israelites were meant to take away from this modest residence that God had prescribed for Himself? How would they have reacted to the fact that the Torah prescribed that the furniture to be placed inside His Mishkan should be little different from that found in any home? Its contents were, two cherubim, reminiscent of little children, a table, a wash basin, pans, jars, bowls, dishes, a menorah, as required in any ancient home to provide light, and a *mizbeach*, an altar, the equivalent of the cooking stove found in every home.

Two messages they would have taken away from this: First, that in Judaism we are meant to attempt to embrace God, not to be in a state of terror of Him. We are encouraged to celebrate our long relationship as His Chosen people, and to feel at home even in fairly modest houses of prayer whose spirit and atmosphere is little different from that of our homes.

We do not need awesome cathedrals, with spires touching the skies, or gold-domed mosques. Ours is a *Bet kneset*, 'a *house* of assembling'. And, just as in a house, every member is loved, and every member has a part to play to ensure its smooth-running, so in the synagogue, every one – man, woman, young adult and child – is a cherished member with expectations, rights, responsibilities, and with an important part to play to foster the spirit and to ensure the security, the smooth-running and social and spiritual development of the community.

The second message of the *Mishkan* as a home, with a lamp, table and cooking utensils, is that, conversely, we are meant to turn our homes into a *Mishkan*, to the extent that even the satisfaction of physical needs can become a sacred act. When we cook only kasher food, we are fulfilling a mitzvah, eating in the manner prescribed by God. When we wash before meals we are doing what the priests did in the *Mishkan* before offering the sacrifices. When we celebrate Shabbat around a traditional table we are symbolizing the sacred table in the *Mishkan*, elevating our eating experience into a sacred act. And when, by the light of the lamp, we read words of Torah, we are bringing the spiritual light of the *Mishkan*'s menorah into our own home.

The two messages we have drawn out from this sidrah may be summarized in this way: we should be at home in synagogue, and we should let synagogue values and traditions find a welcome in our home.

CHAPTER TWENTY-FIVE

Tetzaveh:
Destroying the racism of Amalek

The sidrah *Tetzaveh* generally coincides with Shabbat Parashat Zachor, when we read a special Torah section containing the command to 'remember' what Amalek did to us as we travelled through the desert on our journey out of Egypt: how he attacked the Israelites from the rear, cutting down the stragglers, the slowest and weakest of our people, instead of confronting the regular army that lead at the front (Deuteronomy 25: 17–19). For that cowardly act, the name Amalek remains in Jewish tradition the prime symbol of any heartless and murderous tyrant who indiscriminately attacks defenceless Jews. Indeed, it was Moses himself who coined that association when he stated that, milchamah laShem ba'Amalek middor dor, 'there is a war against Amalek in every generation' (Exodus 17: 16).

We read that special Amalek section from a second Sefer Torah, because it comes so much later in the Torah, in the sidra Ki Teitzei, towards the end of the last book of the Torah, Devarim. To avoid keeping the congregation waiting while we roll the Torah scroll from our sidrah, Tetzaveh, through the rest of the book of Shemot, and the subsequent books of Vayikra, Bemidbar and the sidrot of Devarim – in all, nearly thirty sidrot – we take out two scrolls, and read from the second the portion already rolled to the Zachor passsage.

Now, if the Torah did not specify precisely when we have to make that special act of remembrance of Amalek's dark deed, why do we not wait until we actually arrive at that sidrah, later in the year, which would surely be the most natural time to read it? Why are we in such a hurry to read it just at this particular time in the religious year?

The answer is that this is the most appropriate week of the year, the week leading into Purim. This is because Haman, the villain of the Purim story, showed himself to be a true follower of Amalek, seeking to destroy unarmed, defenceless and law-abiding citizens of his own country. Furthermore, Haman's ancestry is actually traced back in the Book of Esther to Agag, one of the kings of Amalek. Hence we read this portion of Amalek on the Shabbat before Purim to demonstrate the truth of the Torah's prediction that 'there is a war against Amalek in every generation' and that a direct descendant of the Amalekite king who attacked Israel in the desert continued to harbour the identical degree of blind hatred of our people some 900 years later in the country of Persia.

Some seventy years ago another disciple of Amalek, by the name of Adolf Hitler, almost succeeded, where Haman and Amalek failed, to blot out our people; and there are still men of hate – like the Hamas and Hizbollah terrorists and the president of Iran – who have the same Amalekite agenda. How prophetic and hauntingly true are those words of the Torah that the battle against Amalek goes on, uninterruptedly, *middor dor*, 'from generation to generation'.

So how can we best fulfil this Torah command to us to perform a collective act of remembering what Amalek did to us?

One way is by reading in the same week both the special Torah portion exposing Amalek's dark deed, as well as those of Haman from the book of Esther. But that is not all the Torah had in mind. That command is fulfilled by the opening words *Zachor*, 'Remember', 'Mention'. The last two words of that portion, *al tishkach*, 'Do not forget', offer a much more comprehensive challenge to us all, and especially to the younger generation. The challenge is to destroy entirely, root and branch, any trace of Amalek's racism from our society and from the world; to glory in the racial, cultural and religious differences between peoples – which give colour and diversity to the canvas of life – rather than to make such differences a cause for tension, discrimination and violence. The challenge is also to replace indifference to our fellow man with tolerance, friendship and concern.

And that is why we commemorate Purim not only by drowning out the name of Haman when it is mentioned in the Megillah, but also by doing something positive, thoughtful and generous, namely by giving *mishloach manot*, food gifts to others, and *matanot la'evyonim*, donations to the poor. The victory over Amalek, Haman and other racists and anti-Semites will only come about by changing the whole complexion of our unfeeling society and our warring world. And it is up to the younger generation to help achieve all that.

There is no nation that has as developed a concept of the brotherhood of man as ours. The very founder of our faith, Avraham, was given his name to denote that he was *Av hamon goyyim*, the father of a multitude of nations (Genesis 17: 4–5). We do not see ourselves as different to any other race or nation. We see ourselves as brothers, all sons of Abraham. It is the Amaleks, Hamans and anti-Semites that have declared us as different, racially inferior.

But we have weathered that 3,000-year storm, because we have defended ourselves with a shield that is stronger than any missile unleashed against us. The shield of faith, of mutual support, of eternal values, of mercy and charitableness, not only toward our co-religionists but towards all men.

CHAPTER TWENTY-SIX

Ki Tisa:
Putting wealth into perspective

The process of maturing is a matter of learning to put things into perspective. Children have an undeveloped sense of perspective because they have no reservoir of life's experiences from which to draw in order to assess the problems or temptations that newly confront them. One could make the same analogy in the case of people unaccustomed to drinking alcohol who are suddenly plied with drink that they cannot tolerate, or those who, wisely, have never experimented with drugs but who are suddenly persuaded to indulge. The effects can be devastating. The maxim 'forewarned is forearmed' is so true. To be 'forewarned' means to be in a position to pause, put the proposed experience into perspective, and, most important of all, to consider its consequences.

It ought to be possible for teenagers to resist such temptations as drink, drugs and sex, since they only have to consider the numerous cases of young people who have suffered greatly from a lack of self-control in these areas, and who have consequently brought great shame and sadness on themselves and their families often as a result of one brief moment of thoughtlessness.

Yet there is one 'mixed blessing' that is more difficult for anyone – old or young – to resist, namely the allure of wealth. A sense of perspective is certainly essential when it comes to the management of wealth. It is even more difficult than the other three enticements mentioned above, since absolutely everyone around us requires in some measure to seek to acquire it and to experiment with it. We are given spending money at a very early age. We have to work in order to support ourselves and later our families. The cost of buying houses, cars, food, holidays and saving for our old age is so great that people are forever striving to improve their lot and to amass as much money as possible. Hence, unlike the other enticements, the pursuit of wealth – even among the young – is not regarded as a shameful thing. Indeed, even formerly Communist countries, such as Russia and China, are now gearing their economies along capitalistic lines, encouraging investment and profit taking. Judaism appreciated this, and in the 'Blessing over the New Moon' we petition God for *chayim shel osher*, 'a life of wealth'.

And that is what makes the pursuit of it such a difficult matter for thinking youth to grapple with. It is important to appreciate, however, that the issue is not the earning, or even the amassing, of money, but the responsible management of it. The questions to be asked of those blessed with wealth are, is it controlling you or are you controlling it? Are you enabling it to truly 'enrich' your life or simply to make you rich? Has preoccupation with it taken over your life, leaving you no time for family, friends, religious practice, learning Torah, involvement in communal and charitable projects? Have you become obsessed with the acquisition of material things and the company of 'celebrities', rather than with helping to relieve the plight of the less fortunate and maintaining your bond with the 'real people' who have loved and been loyal to you when you were not so rich?

The sidrah *Ki Tisa* opens with the instruction: 'When you count the numbers of the Children of Israel ... they shall contribute half a shekel as a gift to the Lord' (Exodus 30: 11–13). The Midrash on this states that God showed Moses a fiery half-shekel coin and said, 'This is what they shall contribute' (see Rashi on Exodus 30: 13).

The question is asked why the Midrash saw fit to depict God as showing Moses a fiery, rather than just an ordinary, coin? One answer is that God wanted to demonstrate to Israel in a dramatic manner the lesson that money is like fire. In the same way that fire is indispensable to man's survival on the planet, and yet, at the same time, through nuclear combustion, it can also destroy the world, so it is with money. Money can be the source of the greatest blessing if used wisely, but it can also easily destroy those who abuse its benefits.

And this very sidrah proceeds to provide a classical example, in the story of the Golden Calf, of the abuse of wealth and the channelling of it into a destructive end. The idea of enabling the Israelites to take gold, silver and brass jewellery out of Egypt, at the expense of the Egyptians, was so that they would have the wherewithal to contribute toward the construction and furnishings of the holy Sanctuary. But the Israelites offered it with greater alacrity and enthusiasm for the fashioning of an idolatrous symbol. Their wealth, a potential source of holiness, became instead a catalyst for the profane.

In the Hebrew language, the words for 'wealth' and 'happiness' have the identical sound. Both are pronounced *osher*. However, in its meaning of 'wealth', the first letter of *osher* is spelt with an *ayin*, whereas in its meaning of 'happiness' it is spelt with an *alef*. Happiness is a personal state of mind. I can be happy while all around are sad. Hence *osher* meaning 'happiness' is spelt with the *aleph*, connoting the personal 'I'. One cannot allow oneself to be wealthy, however, while everyone else is impoverished. Hence the Hebrew word for 'wealth' commences with an *ayin*. The word *ayin* denotes the human eye, which is constructed to see others, but not itself. This is the Jewish view of wealth: that it is primarily to benefit others even before oneself; to make a difference to the lives of the many; to enrich the community; to alleviate suffering and banish poverty, and to increase the potential for dignity, contentment and self-worth for all the human race.

We pray for the future success, happiness and prosperity of young people, but, above all, that they will manage constructively the wealth with which we hope they will be endowed.

CHAPTER TWENTY-SEVEN

Vayakheil:
The holiness of work

The importance of hard work is expressed at the very beginning of the sidrah Vayakheil where we are told, *Sheishet yamim tei'aseh melachah uvayom ha-shevii yihyeh lachem kodesh, shabbat shabbaton laShem*, 'For six days shall work be done and the seventh day shall be holy unto you, an intense rest in honour of the Lord'. Now, according to some rabbis the first part of the instruction is as much a mitzvah as the second. In other words, it is God's wish not only that we keep the Sabbath, but also that we work hard on the other days of the week (see Midrash Avot de Rabbi Natan 22b).

There is a profound lesson to be taken away from the fact that the Torah inserts into the context of Shabbat a reference to the working week, thereby raising the status of work into the category of holiness. The Torah is telling us here that our working week – our attitude to work as well as the way we work – should be motivated and inspired by the way we observe Shabbat, and that just as Shabbat observance is tightly regulated and hedged in with discipline so must we be equally disciplined and meticulous about our responsibilities at work.

If we are employers we must care deeply for the welfare of our employees. Just as Shabbat affords us time to cement a closer relationship with our family, our friends and the people around us in synagogue, so must we find time at work for those whom we employ. Conversely, if we are employees, we must give of our best and not waste the time for which we are paid or the raw materials and resources supplied to us. Just as on Shabbat, if we observe it properly, it is almost impossible to waste time – since every part of that day is fully taken up, with prayer, study, eating *se'udot* and refreshing our bodies through extra rest – so when we work must we endeavour to make every minute count, and give of our utmost.

We must regard our weekday work or our studies as 'holy', that is, as serving an important and higher purpose, however unskilled be the task or however basic be the level of our study. We should perform our every task, with a sense of purpose, pride and contentment, not as a burden. Just as on Shabbat we derive pleasure from mixing socially with friends and family in the synagogue, so we should find fulfilment throughout the working week in sharing a common enterprise and challenge with fellow students or colleagues.

So the message of the sidrah's apparent 'command' that we work during the other days of the week, in addition to resting on Shabbat, is that we should strive to make every day of our life count. It is not enough to be achievers. We also have to bring the spirit and holiness of Shabbat into everything we do. In that way our working life can also earn us mitzvot when it is conducted according to the ethical and moral values of Judaism, with honesty and fairness, and with sympathy and understanding. Then we will also bring joy and enthusiasm into our work, making the atmosphere all the more pleasurable for ourselves and for all those with whom we work and interact.

CHAPTER TWENTY-EIGHT

Pekudei:
Acquiring skills we never
dreamed we had

The sidrah Pekudei concludes the lengthy account of the construction of the *Mishkan*, the sanctuary in the desert. The
Israelites all generously donated their gold, silver and brass to be
melted down for this project. So generous were they that Moses
had to issue a proclamation telling them to stop contributing as
they had far more raw materials than they required.

While most of the Torah's focus is on the materials, much can
be learnt by considering the designer, the architects and the
builders of the Sanctuary. In Vayakheil they are regularly described
as *chachmat lev*, 'wise-hearted'. It is a strange description since it is
normally the brain, rather than the heart, that is responsible for
skills of that kind.

One of our commentators explains this by pointing out how
amazing it was that any single Israelite could have possessed those
required skills. After all, they had been slaves in Egypt, working
with rough bricks and mortar, not with gold and silver. They had
never been required to measure anything with precision, to
engrave, or to weave and dye materials.

That, says the *Ha'amek Davar* commentary, was where their 'wise
heartedness' was displayed. Most other manual labourers, totally
lacking in any particular creative skill, would have run a mile from
volunteering for such a task. They would have been intimidated
even at the thought of it. But among the Israelites there were some
who were so desperate to participate in that great and sacred project, that they 'sensed wisely' – which is precisely what *chacham lev*

means – that God would never have issued to them a challenge and task that was totally beyond their ability to perform.

They reasoned wisely that all they had to do was their best, and that if it was God's desire to see that project implemented, He would endow them with the required skills, creativity and inspiration.

The boundaries of knowledge would never have been extended in any field if single-minded individuals had not possessed faith in themselves, if they did not have a vision and a dream, a conviction that the process of extending themselves would also lead to an extension of the barriers of knowledge in their chosen fields and the achievement of hitherto undreamed of insights and results.

Before Roger Bannister had completed the four-minute mile for the first time, people had said that it was totally beyond human ability. Within months of his achievement, several other runners managed that feat. What happened was that, instead of accepting what others had said was or was not possible, they began to believe in themselves, in their own ability to extend the boundaries of the possible. A common denominator applicable to all great innovators, indeed to anyone who has made a creative contribution in any particular field, is a relentless belief in themselves, a determination to succeed where others have failed. And that is why records, whether for sailing around the world, climbing the sheerest face of Everest or running around a race track, are still being broken. That is why the impossible regularly becomes the possible, and the miraculous becomes the mundane.

But the mind alone is never enough. To really achieve, we also require the heart, the passion, the total immersion in the challenge we are undertaking. We need to be *chachmat lev*, 'wise of heart'; we need to be so emotionally single-minded that we can shrug off the doubts, the taunts, the derision, sometimes even the dirty tricks, of those who prefer the comfort of the status quo, and who envy the talents of the pioneers and the dreams of the highfliers.

At the beginning of the sidrah Ki Tisa, God commanded the Israelites to contribute a half shekel for the upkeep of their most creative project, the building and furnishing of the Sanctuary. One of the reasons for the half, rather than a whole, shekel lies at the heart of the message we have expounded. It is to indicate that, although we may think we possess only half the required talent, half the knowledge, half the creative skills and half the required resources, yet we cannot know just how far that measure can be extended and augmented if we have faith in God and faith in ourselves. We cannot anticipate just how our half shekel – our small contribution – can join that of countless others, to bring a great project to fulfilment, or how our insights and ideas can link up with those of others to create that which is totally novel, which can contribute immeasurably to the cause of human progress or the benefit of humanity.

None of us is a complete shekel, totally self-sufficient. We all need others to help us achieve our own dreams and to further God's purpose for us, individually and collectively. If we understand that, then we are endowed with chachmat lev, wisdom of the heart, not just wisdom of the mind.

PART THREE
VAYIKRA

CHAPTER TWENTY-NINE

Vayikra:
Sacrifices ancient and modern

Being initiated into the Jewish religious community is not merely a matter of privilege but also of sacrifice and responsibility. And those are the themes of this sidrah which details the sacrifices that were brought in our ancient Sanctuary, and later at the Temples in Jerusalem, for a variety of sins, both personal and communal. There were also special sacrifices to be offered by the leaders of the people, such as the high priests, priests and princes, when they were remiss in their behaviour and failed to act as proper role models for the ordinary folk.

Being an adult means realizing that the rich, the great and the famous are invariably not also 'the good'. This is a lesson that we Jews should not need to be taught, for we have suffered more than any others from the wickedness of the kings, emperors, dictators, prime ministers, popes and religious leaders of the countries which gave us refuge. After helping to bring those countries prosperity, through our hard work, creativity, astuteness and business acumen, they soon resented our success and our presence. They viewed us as a dispensable commodity or a convenient scapegoat when adversity struck, and they exploited, oppressed, murdered and exiled us in most of the countries of Europe.

By a divine miracle, and as a result of countless of those sacrifices we referred to, we returned to our land in 1948, a land to which we never relinquished our title, and never abandoned our dream of returning.

But even after rebuilding a basically desert land, and making it flourish, and after waves of Jewish immigration, the majority of the world's leaders, through the vehicle of the United Nations, still deny us our right of total sovereignty. They swallow the lie that there existed an identifiable Palestinian nation before the State of Israel was founded. Some even accept the preposterous Palestinian propaganda that we Jews never had an ancient state in Israel thousands of years ago, notwithstanding that both the Jewish and Christian Scriptures are set clearly against its background.

There are also a goodly number of Jewish anti-Zionist liberals who ignore the indisputable fact that Israel only came into possession of Sinai (since returned to the Egyptians), Gaza (since returned to the Palestinians) and the West Bank as a result of the fact that the Arabs refused to live in peace with Israel, and attacked her repeatedly with a view to wiping her off the map. They blind themselves to the logic that Israel would be foolhardy to return areas, such as the Golan and the West Bank, until her enemies promise to respect her borders, recognise her sovereignty, and live in peace.

In spite of what happened on 11 September 2001, the world's leaders – other than, notably, President Bush and Mr Blair – simply will not face up to the fact that the terrorist threat to Israel is also a threat to the entire free world. They and their media go along with the absurd notion that, had it not been for Israel's excessively tough response to the Palestinians, global Islamic terrorism would not exist. According to their warped logic, Israel is the one responsible for all the terrorism across the world! Once again, we Jews provide a most convenient scapegoat for the ills of the free world!

At a time like this, no young adult can afford to remain ignorant of, or indifferent to, the struggle that his people and his homeland is facing.

God is the main source of our strength, and its youth is the Jewish nation's backbone. Unlike those who use their youth as missiles, to blow themselves and others up and to be agents of hatred and jihad, Jewish youth are taught the values of peace, love of the stranger, compromise, respect for all those created in the image of God, irrespective of religion, nationality or colour.

And these constitute the dual messages of this sidrah: sacrifice and responsibility – for our people, our religion and our land. Jewish youth are expected to devote themselves to the cause of being ambassadors, spokespeople and fighters for Israel's cause. Where they encounter false propaganda or blind prejudice, they must counter it with courage, protest and firm and informed argument. Where there are lies, they must fearlessly proclaim the truth, and where there is lethargy and indifference on the part of their friends, they must replace it with initiative, energy and action. Jewish adulthood is a call to action, to national as well as spiritual service, to the age-old Jewish battle for survival.

V'im nefesh achat techeta bishgagah, 'And if one soul sins in error' (Leviticus 4: 27). A Chasidic master once said that there can be a righteous man who is nevertheless called a sinner. Namely, if he is *nefesh achat*, 'one soul' – someone who stands alone and indifferent, smug and self-satisfied, and who leaves the cause of the defence of his people to others. Jewish youth have never done that. That is why we regained our homeland, and that is the only way we shall retain it!

CHAPTER THIRTY

Tzav:
Why so many mitzvot

This word *Tzav* means 'command'. A few years ago a storm broke out over Mel Gibson's film on the subject of the crucifixion of Jesus, the origins of Christianity and its stormy relationship with Judaism. One of the principal bones of contention between the two religions in the first century was over this issue of 'commands', of Judaism's manifold laws, practices and rituals to which every young adult commits him or her self.

After his crucifixion by the Romans, Jesus's disciples thought up a most unworthy allegation that the burden of all those 613 mitzvot was actually imposed on Jews by God as a punishment for the simple reason that they had rejected the Christian god and messiah who had come to redeem the world. The fact that this was chronologically absurd – given that the Torah was given about 1,300 years before the Christian era, and therefore could not possibly have related to it – was totally ignored by those misguided evangelists.

The Jewish response, given by a sage called Chananya ben Akashya, was regarded as so basic that it is quoted at the end of the recitation of each chapter of *Pirkei Avot*, the Ethics of the Fathers, which we read on Shabbat afternoons during the summer months. He said, *Ratzah Ha-kadosh baruch hu l'zakot et yisrael lefichach hirbah lahem torah umitzvot*, 'God wanted to lavish as much merit as possible upon Israel, for which reason He gave them a host of mitzvot' (Mishnah Makkot 3: 16). The more we fulfil, the greater the reward we earn.

How wrong those early Christians were. It would have been unthinkable for us Jews ever to have regarded our Torah and miztvot as a burden or, worse, as a punishment. They were always a loving privilege, a blessing, and a sacred and joyous challenge. Every mitzvah we perform is an expression of our love of God, and our loyalty to the way of life that He has mapped out for us. As long as we keep our Torah we will survive as a people. If we neglect it, we lose our identity and perish.

So the call to our young people is clearly to accept their religious duties with love, pride, joy and gratitude, and with the determination that they will never be viewed as a burden. Let the words of Rabbi Chananya ring out: The more we observe, the greater our merit and the greater our blessing.

CHAPTER THIRTY-ONE

Shemini:
The message of 'the strange fire'

The sidrah Shemini records the story of Nadav and Avihu, the two sons of Aaron, who died while being installed into office as priests of the Sanctuary. Their death is explained as due to the fact that 'they offered *strange* fire before the Lord, which He had not commanded' (Leviticus 10: 1). Their punishment was that 'fire came forth from before the Lord and consumed them and they died' (10: 2).

Since time immemorial commentators have struggled to understand this episode and to define the exact nature of that terrible sin of which those two young men, endowed with such promise and leadership potential, were guilty. Particularly mystifying is the fact that they were struck down at that very moment that they were performing a sacred ritual at the altar of the newly consecrated sanctuary. Their thoughts must have been pure, their frame of mind spiritual. Admittedly, they added a ritual – *asher lo tzivah* – 'that God had not commanded', but, after all, religious leaders have been doing just that all down the ages! Had that not been the case we would never have had countless Temple rituals, such as prayer, the singing of psalms and the Succot 'Water Drawing Ceremony', none of which were 'commanded by God!'

We will never know the answer. We can only conjecture. And one of the most interesting suggestions, with considerable relevance for young people today who might be struggling to embrace Orthodox practice, is the one offered by the famous nineteenth-century scholar, the *Netziv* of Volodzin, author of *Ha'amek Davar*. For him, the

eish zarah, 'strange fire', that Nadav and Avihu took is not to be understood literally, but rather as a metaphorical fire. Their intention, he
asserts, was not to reject a divine instruction. Quite the contrary:
They were literally 'on fire', but not with the ritual they were
engaged upon, but rather in blazing the trail of their *own* spirituality.
They were supposed to be participating in an initiation ceremony
of the whole of the priesthood, performing the same rites as their
fellow priests and spiritual leaders, receiving the identical religious
aura and inspiration, and swearing unswerving loyalty to that same
tradition that would embrace, sanctify and unify the entire priesthood fraternity. Instead of furthering thereby the nation's collective
fire and spiritual enthusiasm, they immersed themselves in an *eish
zarah*, a 'strange fire', an external, independently-nurtured, spiritual
experience – *asher lo tzivah ottam* – 'which was not *related to* that which
God had commanded them'.

Their religious intentions were honourable and pure, but they
were misguided. They were not participating in, or promoting, the
nation's native Sinaitic tradition. On the contrary: they were actually
undermining it by seeking out their own independent spiritual
paths, by generating a strange fire, a spirituality rooted in their own
powerful needs and emotions, their own religious yearnings, passions and inclinations, their own experiences, their own perceptions
of the nature of God and his relationship to man.

As such, theirs was actually an act of idolatry. For they were
serving themselves, not God. They were satisfying their own need,
not God's will. They were creating their own, *do-it-yourself*, religion,
and were seeking to go beyond the scope of God's revelation.

One may speculate that this interpretation of the *Netziv* was
inspired by his and his contemporaries' bitter struggle against the
new reforming tradition that was attracting adherents in Europe at
that time. Reform Judaism, according to his perception, was 'the
strange fire that God had not commanded'. It was a man-made
brand of spiritual expression, a non-halachic reinterpretation of
Judaism, rooted in the modern Jew's secular orientation, not in
the original fire of the authentic Sinaitic heritage.

In our day, numerous varieties of 'new age' religious systems
have been created, to the extent that some textbooks on religions

even include Marxism and Scientology in their list of contents. More recently, Madonna's Kabbalism has been added as an independent religious system, totally wrenched from its moorings within Judaism's rabbinic tradition, a mish-mash of ideas, mystical concepts and formulae from a whole range of disjointed and irreconcilable sources. A 'strange fire', if ever there was one!

In the later Sidrah, Acharei Mot, this incident is again referred to, in a way that may be interpreted as a general warning to observant Jews who glory in their perceived proximity to God. After the reference to the death of Aaron's two sons, 'God said to Moses, "Tell Aaron your brother that he should not enter the Sanctuary at all times ..."' (Leviticus 16: 2). This is a caution against religious exhibitionism, and the feigning of familiarity with God.

God has also to be allowed His space. He does not wish to share heaven with man. He wants man to celebrate life and to be active within general society. He wants him to enjoy the blessings of nature, of education, of culture and creative endeavour. He wants man to live in the real world, a place of temptation and distraction, where his moral mettle can really be put to the test, but where he can also gain immense reward for overcoming all those beguiling obstacles.

Torah has to be wedded to life. It is life's natural element. It is not meant to be studied in a vacuum or lived in a hot house of pure spirituality, divorced from the world and its concerns.

This is a lesson that those young people who have come fresh to Orthodoxy should take to heart. They should never cut themselves off from their less observant family, imagining that they have now become 'too holy' to fraternize with them. Neither should they sever their contacts with their non-observant friends. If their faith is authentically strong, they will influence the latter for good far more easily than they themselves will be influenced by them in the other direction. Finally, they should not cut themselves off from their mainstream Orthodox community to join Charedi, Ultra-Orthodox, separatist communities. They should not forget the spiritual debt they owe the community for the early religious education that it provided, and for the Jewish life, values and sense of identity that it nurtured. That is a debt that they should feel obliged to repay.

CHAPTER THIRTY-TWO

Tazria-Metzorah:
Why girls reach religious
maturity before boys

The sidrah Tazria commences with the subject of childbirth and the sacrifices to be offered by the new mother at the Sanctuary.

Woman was given the special privilege of carrying and nurturing the growing foetus and bringing it safely into the world. Her glorious primary role at that formative period of the baby's existence cannot be denied; and hence, although Adam was given his name 'because he was formed from the ground (adamah)', his wife was called chavah, 'because she was the mother of all life (chayyim)'.

But the status of woman goes beyond her biological role, and she also seems to have been endowed with a more advanced spiritual and educational growth-capacity. How else do we explain the fact that Judaism viewed girls as responsible adults, fully able to discharge their religious duties and possessing mature spiritual insights, at the age of 12, whereas boys were perceived as requiring a further year to reach that level?

This may be viewed as quite uncharacteristic of Judaism, which in other respects entrusts to men the prime duty of studying Torah and obligating them to perform so many more mitzvot than women. So how did it come about that girls are regarded as so much ahead of men as regards their religious maturity?

It may have to do with the fact that mother Eve displayed a far greater thirst for knowledge and moral discretion than her husband, Adam, and that her quest for knowledge actually preceded his. Indeed, if not for woman, man might never have evolved into the uniquely intelligent being that he became, with a natural curiosity for understanding the physical and spiritual worlds.

It was mother Eve, after all, who enticed Adam to eat of the fruit of the Tree of Knowledge of good and evil. Adam was content to remain in ignorance, to take God's prohibition at face value, to sleep and dream all day long in a Garden of Eden. Eve suspected that God's prohibition may well have been nothing more than a test to see just what value they would place on the acquisition of knowledge. Had God really wanted to prevent Adam from eating of that special tree He could have totally removed it out of sight, made it unattractive to them, or coiled a poisonous serpent around it. Who knows? Maybe that was precisely the role of the serpent in that story.

God surely knew that His humans could, and would, disobey Him, eat of the tree, and gain knowledge, discrimination, freedom of thought and action. So it must have been God's plan all along that one of them would find it just too alluring. And who was it that thirsted most for knowledge? It was Eve, woman. She was prepared to suffer the consequences, even of disobeying God's will, in order that her husband should be more than a dreamer. She enabled him, and the human race, to be, in the words of the psalmist, *Vat'chasreyhu me'at mei'Elokim*, 'just a little lower than the angels' (Psalm 8: 6). Without woman, man would have been just another species of animal.

That trail-blazing role of woman in the acquisition of knowledge may well have been responsible for her having been regarded as worthy of entering the ranks of the adult Jewish community a year earlier than her male counterparts. It will be her particular noble task, when she has children of her own, to nurture within them in their infant years that love of learning that mother Eve passed down as a heritage to all the members of her sex.

CHAPTER THIRTY-THREE

Acharei Mot:
Saying 'sorry!' to God and man

The Sidrah Acharei-Mot deals with the institution of Yom Kippur, the most sacred day in our religious calendar, referred to elsewhere as *Shabbat Shabbaton*, which, translated literally, means 'a rest of rest', or 'the ultimate rest' (Leviticus 23: 32). Whereas on an ordinary Shabbat we desist from work and turn our minds to other ways of sacred celebration, such as by having three meals (*shalosh Seudot*), resting for a while, socially interacting with family and friends – all in addition to attending shul, which at one level also provides a fairly relaxed, social experience – Yom Kippur is entirely different, providing none of those other pleasures and distractions. It is truly *Shabbat Shabbaton*, the 'ultimate rest', the day whereon we 'rest from' all physical and mental distractions, focusing our minds exclusively on the task of prayer, petition and introspection.

Most of us come away from a day of fasting and prayer like Yom Kippur with a feeling of spiritual elation, having made our peace with God for the many positive and negative miztvot of the Torah that we have neglected throughout the year. We have probably also made a mental justification for our neglect of so many mitzvot on the basis that we lead such busy and stressful lives that we simply do not have time to perform them all. I have heard some people even justify their sins on the grounds that, with so many really evil people around, perpetrating real violence and gross immorality, their own misdeeds must surely be considered by God as quite insignificant!

Let us focus on just two of the scores of messages that may be derived from aspects of the Yom Kippur observance.

First, the issue of making our peace with God. The question we must ask is whether that is the sole objective of the day? A glance at a verse in this sidrah provides the answer: 'For on this day shall atonement be made for you to cleanse you; from all your sins before the Lord shall you be clean' (Leviticus 16: 30). The great sage, Rabbi Eleazar ben Azariah, pointed out that the phrase to be emphasized in this verse is 'from all your sins *before the Lord* shall you be clean' – but for sins against your fellow man you cannot be cleansed until you have personally begged his forgiveness for any wrong perpetrated (Mishnah Yoma 8: 9).

As a congregational rabbi for forty years, I have seen many a Yom Kippur pass with some individuals in my community never having even attempted to say 'sorry!' for wrongs they have inflicted. They have allowed years and years to pass, nursing grievances, sustaining ill will, harbouring grudges and jealousies, refusing to pay debts or to fulfil promises to members of their family or to charity. They have been fervent in their Yom Kippur prayers to God, but totally silent in their petitions to their neighbour. How foolish could they have been to imagine that God could be deceived into believing that they have put their wrongdoing behind them. After all, did not God Himself demand of us, *V'ahavta l'rei'acha kamocha*, 'You shall love your neighbour as yourself' (Leviticus 19: 18)? How, then, can we insult, humiliate, speak evil about, and cheat, our neighbour, and still expect God to view us charitably and forgivingly?

So the first message to take away from the Yom Kippur theme of this sidrah is that God cannot be hoodwinked! He is waiting for us to make our peace with, and offer forgiveness to, our friends and associates before He is prepared to even consider granting pardon for our religious shortcomings.

The second Yom Kippur message derives from the opening verses wherein God makes it clear that Aaron, the High Priest, was not to enter the Holy of Holies more than once a year to beg God for atonement for the nation (Leviticus 16: 2). There is another important message here: children are conditioned to saying 'sorry!' at the drop of a hat. This is because, whenever they have hurt another child or done something wrong, they are sternly told by their parents to 'say sorry!'

The little child can be forgiven for thinking that as long as he or she says 'sorry!' everything is forgiven. It takes time until it dawns on the child that saying 'sorry!' is but a formality, a token of acceptance that one was in the wrong, and that the important thing is to try hard not to repeat the act again. This is expressed very clearly in the Mishnah: 'Whoever says, "I shall sin and then repent; I shall sin and then repent again", will not be granted pardon on Yom Kippur' (Mishnah Yoma ad loc).

Aaron, the High Priest, was taught this lesson very clearly. By allowing him to enter the Holy of Holies only once a year, on Yom Kippur, to make atonement for Israel, God was saying, in essence,

> You have but one chance to say 'sorry!' for sins committed against Me or against your neighbour. If your prayers and petitions for forgiveness were not whole-hearted, and if you excluded certain sins or certain people from your determination to right the wrongs, then I do not wish to hear from you until next year. If I decide at any time during that period to exact punishment for such a category of sins that you have committed, then you have lost your chance of avoiding retribution. I give you one window of opportunity each year. Don't squander it, and don't keep bothering Me!

So this second message is for us to seize the opportunity to patch up quarrels, to say a sincerely-meant 'sorry!' in time for Yom Kippur, and to attempt to conduct all our relationships with both God and fellow man in a way that we will have no need to say 'sorry!' again.

CHAPTER THIRTY-FOUR

Kedoshim:
Sex, restraint and marriage

Young people become aware all too soon of all the crime and violence that our society breeds. They read of it in the papers, see it reported and dramatized on television, and frequently suffer it personally or in their circle of family or friends. We read of schoolchildren being attacked or racially abused, of a high proportion of youth carrying and using knives, and robbing and even killing people to provide money to feed their drug addiction.

Many will also be aware of acquaintances indulging in sexual activity, of young girls becoming pregnant, having abortions, endangering themselves morally and physically, as well as ruining any chances they may have had of building a carefree and successful future for themselves. This is all the result of casting off restraint, of refusing to wait a while before enjoying pleasures that were created for a human happiness exclusively linked to a commitment of responsibility.

That is why Judaism is so insistent that sex be exclusively reserved for the marriage relationship, wherein it becomes an expression of true love and of total partnership in all the experiences of life. In marriage, the person with whom sex is enjoyed has already committed him- or herself to a lifetime of sharing the good and the difficult times, sharing everything that the other possesses, all their hopes and ambitions, all the joys and milestones of life. He or she is not just using the other's body for selfish pleasure and reserving the right to terminate the relationship and look for another partner if and when boredom sets in. The married couple know that their love is driven by far more than just physical attraction, and that, with every passing year and shared family experience, the relationship and reliance on each other deepens and expands. They know that their marriage is intended to bring them closer not only to each other but also to God, and that the home they have established is intended to be a sanctuary, a place where Judaism's home rituals can be joyfully celebrated and experienced, and where they can find peace and tranquillity from the turbulence of modern life.

One of the important objectives of the married couple's sexual relationships is also the creation of children who will be conceived in true love and brought up in a happy and carefree environment, children for whom the home will be an educational, inspirational and protective cocoon, a place of laughter, love and learning. How cruel it is, therefore, to bring unwanted children into the world, those born as a result of 'an unfortunate accident'. In most cases those children grow up bearing the psychological scars of that situation, especially if their mother ends up as a single parent. And that is, alas, the situation that confronts the majority of unmarried women who bear children.

The opening verse of the sidrah *Kedoshim* establishes that God requires that we exhibit restraint in the sphere of our physical appetites and sexual desires, and that restraint is the road leading to holiness and happiness. After all, God was the one who first designed us and implanted within our bodies the capacity to derive intense physical pleasure – from good food, wine, music, sports and leisure activities, as well as from sex. But His objective was that those pleasures should be part of an integrated mosaic called 'life', not indulged in as individual and disjointed ends in themselves. He has commanded us to work for six days, and to enjoy rest on the Sabbath. He has prescribed even within marriage certain restrictions on sexual relationships during the period of the menstrual cycle when the woman has the opportunity to recover from its effects. He has blessed us with countless foodstuffs, but He has also restricted us to those that are 'kasher'. He has allowed us the joy of eating meat, but has imposed a subsequent waiting period before we may have dairy foods. He has granted us the pleasure of eating and drinking on most days of the year, but has restricted the intake of food on fast days such as Yom Kippur. And so the list goes on. Our lives partake, therefore, of times and situations when we have to exhibit restraint and self-discipline, acknowledging that, in the words of the psalmist, *LaShem ha'aretz umlo'ah*, 'The earth and its bounty belong to God' (Psalm 24: 1).

The ancient Israelite farmer also had to demonstrate restraint, and hold back from exploiting every ounce of vitality and produce from his fields. Hence every seven years he had to observe a *shemittah*, allowing the field to remain fallow and regain its strength. That also was a demonstration that we may be the temporary owners of the field, but God's title is paramount. It is only by His grace and with His blessing that nature delivers up its harvests.

Kedoshim tihyu – 'Be holy'(Leviticus 19: 2). The rabbis do not define this as a command to pray all day, to seek to scale the heights of heaven, to become nazarites and deny ourselves the pleasures of life. Their definition of *kedoshim*, 'holiness' – as quoted by *Rashi* – is *hevu perushim min ha'arayot umin ha'aveirah*, 'Exhibit restraint in your moral behaviour, and keep aloof from relationships that are forbidden by the Torah' – or frowned upon by any decent society.

This message has always been central to the life of observant Jews. Family life has always been the key to our survival and cohesion, and it is underpinned by moral behaviour, integrity and responsibility. This explains why the very next verse in the sidrah states: *Ish immo v'aviv tiyra'u* – 'A man should revere his father and mother'(verse 3). We should abide by their values and standards, and do nothing to bring them shame or disgrace.

This is a call that young people especially need to hear if the moral fabric of society is to hold together in the future.

CHAPTER THIRTY-FIVE

Emor:
Making every day count

The sidrah *Emor* contains the *Parashat Ha-Moadim*, a survey of all the festivals of the year (Leviticus ch. 23). An important message for young people may be derived from its description of the *Omer* period and the command that we count the forty-nine days from Pesach, when the barley harvest was gathered in and brought to the Temple as an offering, until Shavuot when the later-ripening wheat harvest and the *bikkurim*, the early fruits, were harvested and also brought ceremoniously to the Temple.

The message derives from the strange fact that the Torah prescribed that we count the period *between* the gathering in of two harvests, rather than the period *leading up to* the first harvest. After all, counting is a way of demonstrating our excitement and anticipation of something unique that we are looking forward to. It would surely make greater sense, therefore, for the ancient Israelite farmer to have counted for forty-nine days *before Pesach*, to symbolize his joyful anticipation of the first harvest of the newly-ripening produce of the new agricultural year. Why only start counting *after* that first Pesach harvest, in anticipation of the second harvest at Shavuot? Surely, the farmer, with a bumper barley harvest being brought in before his eyes on Pesach, would hardly feel, to the same extent, that great sense of novelty, excitement and anticipation in the face of the next harvest to be brought in around Shavuot? After all, he had already savoured the sweet taste of success and the sense of security and achievement that accompanies it! The Shavuot first fruits were really the icing on an already-baked cake.

One message that we can derive from this arrangement is not to be satisfied with any single achievement in life but always to work at self-improvement and ever higher levels of success. If we ever thought that we had reached the summit of our ability with one success, we would have nothing more to strive for, and would just sleep all day. We would have no challenges, no reason to study further, to work hard, to develop our knowledge and skills, nothing to save up for and invest in. Life would lose all its tension, all its excitement, all its scope for greater opportunity.

So we do not count the Omer prior to Pesach. We count it *after* the Pesach harvest, to teach us not to rest on our laurels, not to be content with the realization of just one dream, but to use every success as the springboard for the next challenge, for extending our horizons more and more.

The message of the counting of the Omer is that we should not merely count days, but also make every day count; that we should not rely on one-off achievements, but build on them and work toward an entire life of achievement and dedication to the needs of the community and to those less fortunate than ourselves.

CHAPTER THIRTY-SIX

Behar/Bechukotai:
Shemittah and our philosophy
of life

The sidrah Behar opens with a reference to the laws of Shemittah, the seventh year when the land had to lie uncultivated and at rest. So important is this institution that in the following sidrah, Bechukotai (which is joined to Behar twice as frequently as they are read as separate sidrot), we find a further reference to it. In the latter case it is mentioned as a divine command, the neglect of which would cause Israel to be invaded and taken into captivity:

> And I shall make your land desolate ... and will scatter you among the nations ... and your cities shall be devastated. Then shall the land be repaid, through being desolate, for the [years of] rest [of which it was deprived]. When you are [captive] in your enemy's land, your own land shall be repaid for all the periods of rest (that it missed). (Leviticus 26: 34–35)

This law of Shemittah differs from most other mitzvot in the Torah which are classified into either positive or negative laws. Positive laws are those such as, 'Keep the Sabbath day holy', 'Put on tzitzit' and 'love your neighbour as yourself'. Examples of negative laws are, 'Do not murder', 'Do not steal', 'Do not delay to pay a hired man his wages'.

The Shemittah law, prohibiting work during the seventh year, is unique in that, for a period, it converts a permitted – even recommended – activity into a forbidden one. Work in the field is not only necessary for livelihood but also provides a framework for the fulfilment of many other mitzvot relating to agriculture, such as the giving of tithes from one's produce, as well as support of the poor, the widow and the orphan. For six of the seven-year agricultural cycle it is a worthy means of earning a livelihood, yet in the seventh year any work on the field is suddenly prohibited. This means that the farmer actually fulfils a mitzvah through *not* working!

The nearest parallel to this is the institution of Shabbat and the festivals, whereby by ceasing work we also fulfil a mitzvah. However, even they do not constitute quite as dramatic a mitzvah as Shemittah, since on those days in the year work was never permitted. They were always singled out as holy days in the calendar when working for a livelihood was forbidden, whereas the Shemittah, as we have observed, actually converts an entire working year into a period of inactivity.

Judaism was clearly not satisfied with us devoting a Sabbath day each week to spiritual matters, or taking off a couple of weeks for the observance of Pesach and Succot, and a couple of days each for Shavuot and Rosh Hashanah. That is not really a major sacrifice. It does not significantly affect a person's financial situation. But for members of an agricultural society to give up one entire year's income out of seven, that is truly a very great sacrifice. That is truly a meaningful demonstration of faith that God would not let them starve, but would provide extra blessing and income throughout the six years of activity. It was also a demonstration by the farmer that he and his family fully accepted the affirmation of the psalmist, *LaShem ha-aretz umlo'ah*, 'To the Lord belongs the earth and its fullness' (Psalm 24: 1). For the duration of that entire year the farmer demonstrated that the land did not belong to him, but to God.

In addition, the Shemittah year offered a wonderful opportunity to the Judean farming communities to devote themselves from morning till night to the study of their heritage, to prayer, to the practice of good deeds and to having extended quality time with their families. The religious leaders would undoubtedly have organized adult learning programmes for all levels. The farmers generally had to work uninterruptedly from morning till night, in fields remote from the centres of learning and with little time anyway to attend school. Were it not for the Shemittah they would have been doomed to permanent illiteracy. But the Shemittah year offered a golden opportunity for them to fill in the wide gaps in their literacy skills and religious education, as well as for the observances that they had neglected. They were now able to spend as much time as it took in the proper exercise of prayer, rather than having to gabble a quick *Shema* or *Amidah* out in the fields.

What are the messages to be taken from this? Well, first and foremost, the emphasis that Judaism places on education. History does not record a single country whose entire population was expected to abandon the race for material prosperity and concentrate for a whole year on spiritual and educational pursuits. Not surprisingly, we Jews are famed for making education, religious and secular, our chief priority. In earlier times, parents went without food in order to pay the fees for their children to attend good schools and colleges. So the first message for the young adult is to take his or her school and Torah studies seriously.

A second, and most important, message to be learnt from the Shemittah institution is to remember that, as in the case of the ancient Judean farmer, it is never too late to make up for early educational opportunities that were not fully utilized. Just as the farmers seized the opportunity offered for a refresher course in learning every seventh year, so should we endeavour to make up for a Jewish education that might have been lacking in depth and inspiration. Many male and female students do just that in their 'gap year', and spend the most interesting and stimulating year of their lives at yeshivot or seminaries in Israel. Most of them beg their parents to let them stay on an extra year before returning home to commence their university education, claiming that they never realized how profoundly interesting, exciting and fulfilling was the study of their faith and religious literature, coupled with the experience of living a vibrant religious and social life.

The third and final message to be learnt from the Shemittah institution is that becoming rich is not the 'be-all and end-all' of life. Few of the ancient Judean farmers became rich – just as British farmers have to receive a subsidy from the government in order to continue to produce the non-profit-making grain we require – and yet they were prepared to invest an entire year's income in their own and their family's spiritual and educational development.

They realized – and so should we – that money is not an end in itself. There is no point in amassing money if the only thing to benefit is the bottom line of the bank balance. That is a mere paper profit. Money has to be used for truly enriching our own lives, for providing ourselves with the time to pursue extra cultural, educational and spiritual opportunities. It also has to be used for making such opportunities available to others and for improving the lot of the less fortunate.

An entire philosophy of life is contained in that single institution of the Shemittah. Go and learn!

PART FOUR

BEMIDBAR

CHAPTER THIRTY-SEVEN

Bemidbar:
When and when not
to be a protester

If we look at the ten sidrot that comprise the current book of Bemidbar, we see that eight of them contain themes of dissatisfaction and protest. In the Sidra *Naso*, we have a situation where a man protests publicly – and probably unjustly – about his wife's moral conduct. In *Beha'alotcha*, the Israelites protest against the lack of variety in their diet of heavenly manna, and they lust after meat. In *Shelach lecha*, they weep and protest against God, preferring to believe the false report of the spies rather than the promise of God to bring them into a land flowing with milk and honey.

In the sidrah *Korach*, we have the story of a large-scale rebellion against Moses and Aaron, and Korach's protest that 'all the congregation are equally holy', and that Moses and Aaron had no special claim to a higher spiritual or leadership status.

In the sidrah *Chukkat*, the Israelites protest unworthily at the temporary lack of water, and claim that God has brought them to die in the desert. They protest justifiably, on the other hand, at the King Sichon's refusal to allow them to pass peacefully through his territory on the way to the Promised Land.

In the sidrah *Balak* we have an off-stage example of protest, with the king of Moab remonstrating vehemently with the heathen prophet, Bilaam, whom he had hired to curse Israel, at the latter's seeming inability to disobey the Israelite God. Bilaam ended up blessing, rather than cursing, Israel.

In the sidrah *Pinchas* we have another protest, though this time a justifiable one, by the daughters of Tzelafchad, who argued against the unfairness of the laws of inheritance which, until that time, only permitted land to be passed on to male heirs.

In the Sidrah *Mattot*, Moses protests against the fact that the Israelite army had disregarded orders and spared the lives of the Midianite women who would ultimately prove to be an immoral scourge to the nation. The tribes of Reuven, Gad and half Menasseh also protested at having to take up an inheritance in the Promised Land proper, which, they alleged, would not be large enough for their vast flocks.

We Jews clearly have a very well-honed critical faculty; and we are almost as critical of our own leaders as we are of our enemies.

The message of this book of Bemidbar, the book of protest, is twofold. First, in general, it is a call to us to avoid becoming professional protesters. There are too many of those around! We should rather look for ways in which we can contribute towards remedying shortcomings, defusing tensions, smoothing away misunderstandings and restoring peace and harmony, whether in one's social circle, one's family life, in one's professional, business or communal life, if not even beyond, in society at large.

The second message is a call to young people to become protesters when they see an injustice being perpetrated, the weak being downtrodden, the poor going hungry, the stranger being exploited, their own people's cause being misrepresented, their religious rights being compromised, and their right to a secure land of their own being violently contested and undermined.

We have to know when and when not to protest!

CHAPTER THIRTY-EIGHT

Naso:
The name at the top of the list

Vayehi beyom kallot Mosheh lehakim et ha-mishkan, 'And it was on the day that Moses finished setting up the Sanctuary' (Numbers 7: 1). The Midrash finds it astonishing that the establishment of the Mishkan is attributed to Moses, when he actually had no part in its actual design and construction. That was the task of a man called Betzalel whose artistic creativity and architectural skills are regularly and readily acknowledged in the last three sidrot of the book of Exodus, in the description of the design, manufacture and equipping of that Sanctuary. Betzalel is described as having been endowed by God with *chokhmah tevunah v'da'at,* 'experience, powers of assessment and skills' (Exodus 31: 3; 35: 31). Why, then, was the setting up of the Sanctuary attributed to Moses and not properly credited to Betzalel?

In explanation, the Midrash quotes a relevant verse from the book of *Kohelet,* Ecclesiastes (2: 21): *Ki yesh adam she'amalo bechochmah* – 'There is a man whose toil is invested with wisdom'. This, says the Midrash, refers to Betzalel. However, the continuation of the verse: *Ul'adam shelo amal boh yitnennu chelko* – 'But to the one who has not toiled he gives the credit' – refers to Moses, who did nothing for the Sanctuary and yet, in our sidrah, receives all the credit for it (see Midrash Bemidbar Rabba and Rashi ad loc).

The same, unfair situation occurs again in relation to the Temple in Jerusalem which is always identified as the Temple of Solomon, whereas, in reality, it was King David who did all the *amal,* the toil, by way of purchasing the site, preparing the detailed plans, ingathering all the gold, silver and brass, transporting all the great stone building blocks, and even selecting the precious gems for the High Priest's breastplate. It was David, therefore, who enabled his son, Solomon, to proceed immediately to its construction, for which reason, in a communication to David, God refers to the future Temple as 'your house' (2 Samuel 7: 16). Yet his pioneering contribution is subordinated to that of his son, Solomon, after whom the Temple is universally named.

It is little different today. A recent fire, which destroyed a whole warehouse of some very mediocre works of modern art, illustrates how some people are lucky enough to find sponsors to promote their work and to catapult them to fame, while other truly great and gifted artists may live out their lives in comparative obscurity. Similarly, there have been many people who have donated large sums of money in order to obtain royal honours (a practice that has now been stopped), while other sincerely dedicated volunteers, who gave their lives to charitable, welfare or educational causes, were frequently overlooked. In academic life also, when scientific or medical papers are published in journals it is generally the professor's name that appears as the prime author of the research, when, in reality, it is more often his less senior staff and researchers who have done all the work. One is reminded of the old music-hall ditty lamenting that injustice: 'It's the poor wot gets the blame. / It's the rich wot gets the gravy. / Ain't it all a bleeding shame!'

But publicity is superficial, and Betzalel did not mind for one moment that Moses was the one to receive the ultimate honour of being associated with the establishment of the Sanctuary. Betzalel had played his God-given part, and he could take enormous pride in the fact that God had employed his artistic and creative skills in such a sacred enterprise. Indeed, he was very conscious of the fact that it was God who had endowed him with his artistic genius precisely so that it could be employed in the design, construction and furnishing of His holy residence. Betzalel knew that he was but the agent of God, and that Moses was the one who possessed the authentic *ruach ha-kodesh*, divine spirit. In the same way, King David did not mind that he had to take a back seat, and that, although he had done all the groundwork – the planning and *shlepping* for the Temple – it was his son, Solomon, who would live to dedicate it and whose name would be forever associated with that great spiritual enterprise.

On a Bar or Bat Mitzvah weekend, the young person is in the full glare of the limelight. All the excitement and celebration revolves around them. But once that weekend is over, they know they will have to accommodate themselves to a different, and more natural, situation, where they must vacate the stage and join the ranks of countless other young people who are left with the religious responsibility, but without all the hype that went with it on that great occasion.

Indeed, it is only in subsequent years, when the memory of their great day has faded somewhat, that their performance as a true Bar or Bat Mitzvah will be properly evaluated. For that status is not merely a matter of learning a portion to sing or a *dvar Torah* to declaim. It is a matter of living each day as a proud and observant Jew or Jewess, of being content to serve worthy causes whether or not their name appears on the notepaper. It is then that the wider and more challenging test of an adult Jew will be administered, the test of walking humbly with God, of following in their family's proud tradition of service to the community, to the Jewish heritage, to the cause of Israel, and to living a life of integrity and Jewish responsibility.

It is important to remember that the status of Bar or Bat Mitzvah is not removed on the Sunday night when the band are boxing away their instruments and the amplifiers with which they have deafened most of the older guests! Then it has only just begun. It is a lifetime status which is shared with millions of adult co-religionists all over the world. We are all part of that great, collective national and religious endeavour. We are all responsible for each other. We all have a part to play: some in leadership roles, others as vital fieldworkers. And if it is only the names of the leaders that are included in the roll of honour – so be it! In the words of a great sage: *Echad ha-marbeh v'echad ha-mam'it, ubilvad sheyechavein et libbo l'avinu shebashamayim.* 'It matters not whether one achieves much or little, providing that he directs his heart to our Father in Heaven' (Tal. Berachot 5b). He knows how hard we have worked and how sincerely dedicated we are. In His book, the names of the fieldworkers may even precede those of the leaders!

CHAPTER THIRTY-NINE

Beha'alotchah:
The lasting effects of a
Bar/Bat Mitzvah

This sidrah records a curious story about two people with curious names, Eldad and Medad. The Israelites had murmured against Moses and God regarding the terribly restricted diet of manna that was available to them in the desert. They craved after the 'fleshpots of Egypt', and the incomparable cuisine that they claimed to have enjoyed there. Knowing full well that he did not have sufficient animals to provide meat for the entire nation, Moses is at his wit's end, and he turns to God, saying, 'I can't cope on my own any more with this rabble!' (Numbers 11: 14)

God responds by telling Moses that he should select seventy elders to help him sort out the problem, but that the downside would be that some of Moses' unique spirituality would be removed from him and shared among those elders. The result of this would be that they would subsequently be endowed with the prophetic quality and inspiration required to lead God's people.

A strange thing happened. The Torah states that, as soon as the spirit descended on those elders, *va-yitnabu v'lo yasafu*, 'they starting prophesying, but did so no more' (11: 25).

Now, two of those who were originally chosen, Eldad and Medad, refused to accept their appointment. Because of their saintliness and great humility they felt unworthy to be elevated in Moses' new honours list, and they did not join the others at the appointed place outside the camp. But rather than viewing them as rebels, God actually bestowed on them also the full measure of prophetic quality, and they found themselves prophesying, *ba-machaneh*, in the camp, among the ordinary folk (11: 26).

Joshua, Moses' trusted assistant was outraged, and he ran to Moses and breathlessly told him of the terrible thing that had occurred. Joshua clearly viewed this as an act of rebellion against Moses' leadership. He could barely utter a mere four words: *Eldad uMedad mitnab'im ba-machaneh*, 'Eldad and Medad are prophesying in the camp!' After composing himself somewhat, he added another three words, *Adoni Mosheh k'la'eim*, 'My lord, Moses, imprison them!'

Moses' response summed up his innate humility. He turned to Joshua, saying, 'Why are you so jealous for my honour?' *Umiy yitein kol am Ha-Shem nevi'im*, 'If only God's entire people were prophets, recipients of His spirit!' (11: 29)

There are a number of messages to be derived from this story, primarily that of the nature of authentic humility. Moses was not in the least threatened by the prospect of others sharing his spirit, being invested with authority, and benefiting the nation. As we go through life we will inevitably, and sadly, encounter some people who put their own ambition, their own wish for the limelight, for honour, public acclaim, influence and power, before the cause, before the desire simply to serve, in whatever capacity they can, as a duty, a *mitzvah*, a privilege. The message is to keep one's distance from such people. They do the community no honour by their service.

The second message, derived from the actions of Eldad and Medad, is also associated with leadership. This is the message of misplaced humility. They were certainly spiritually gifted men, men who should have put their knowledge, their passion for God, their love of Israel, their organizational talents, at the disposal of the nation. But they lacked self-esteem, as had Moses himself initially, when he was told by God to go down to Egypt and become the redeemer of Israel.

When one senses that one is chosen, that one can contribute of one's talents to the betterment of the community or society, it is an ungenerous act to hold back from leadership through a misplaced sense of humility. God in fact made this point by investing the two with that prophetic spirit 'in the camp', where it was misplaced and secularized, instead of in the select company of their brethren. Their punishment was that their authentic humility was now publicly misconstrued – by Joshua and probably the majority of Israel – as an unacceptable act of exhibitionism. Not surprisingly, we never hear of Eldad and Medad again. They lost that spiritual ecstasy and exaltation which had originally prompted them to attain to the level of prophets.

There is a parallel here with the emotions that are generated in the hearts of so many Bar and Bat Mitzvahs. For some the occasion is one of religious ecstasy, akin to that experienced by those seventy elders. For most it is an indescribable feeling of excitement, joy and pride in their faith. But the most important question is not how they feel on that sacred day, but how they will feel the next day, the next month, the next year? Will it be a very short-lived ecstasy, as was the case with those elders, or will it remain with them throughout their life? These are some of the challenges contained in this Sidrah.

CHAPTER FORTY

Beha'alotchah:
Don't be a murmurer!

One of the messages to be extracted from this sidrah is about values and priorities. I refer to the story about the manna, the heavenly food that God sent each day to feed and nourish the Israelites and to stop them dying of starvation in the bleak desert.

But the Israelites could not appreciate just what a miracle was being performed for them, and they started to hallucinate about all the delicious delicacies that they dreamed they had enjoyed in Egypt. We know that they had to make do with matzah, bread of affliction, and that they had no money to purchase delicacies; but when *they* looked back on their time in Egypt, they suddenly had this idealistic vision of sitting at banquets of the finest and freshest fish, fruit and vegetables. And they came murmuring against Moses and crying and lamenting outside their tents.

This is what we mean by misguided values and priorities. What did they expect in the desert? Fish, fruit and vegetables? Not for a moment did they face the reality that they were on their way, through a desert, to the achievement of their freedom, and that, to reach the Promised Land, when they would indeed enjoy all those delicacies, they had, of necessity, to endure some inconvenience. It is like a Jewish prisoner in jail complaining that the authorities were not ordering a Kasher Chinese take-away for him! The Israelites should have been more than satisfied that food of any kind was provided for them. Perhaps this is what our rabbis meant when they said, *Eisehu ashir, ha-sameach b'chelko,* 'Who is a wealthy man? He that is content with what he has' (Ethics of the Fathers 4: 1).

Our present generation is probably the least content of any generation in the history of man. No one seems satisfied with what they have, because no sooner have they acquired it when an updated, more sophisticated, greater capacity version hits the market. We have no relationship with the things, and often the people, around us. We are the 'throw away society'. So no one is totally content with what they are given, with what they achieve, with the designer goods they are wearing. Everyone is on the look out for the updated version, for the way they can be one-up on their friends and neighbours. No one has the time to enjoy what they have, because no sooner than they have unwrapped it, when someone is advertising or telling them about what they are missing.

That is the message to take away from this episode of the murmurers.

It teaches us to be content with, and enjoy to the full, what we have; to share what we have with others; to value the things in life that are of eternal value, and that do not evaporate with changing fashion. It calls on us to value human beings, value family, value knowledge, value friendship, value values – of kindness, of truth, of tolerance, of love. Above all, to value our relationship with God, with Torah, with Israel, and to be a *same'ach b'chelko*, someone who is content with what he or she possesses, whatever its size or value, and who never envies the possessions of others.

CHAPTER FORTY-ONE

Shelach-Lecha:
Resisting the influence of the
wrong kind of friends

Joshua was Moses' most faithful right-hand man, never leaving his side and, eventually, taking over from him as leader and commander-in-chief of the Israelite army. It was Joshua who led the Hebrews into the Promised Land.

But Joshua – *Yehoshua* – was not his original name. That was simply *Hoshe'a*, which means 'Save!' But just before Moses sent him out, as a member of the delegation of twelve men charged with spying out the land of Israel, he suddenly had a sense of prophetic intuition that this would be a hazardous mission, and that some of the other spies would try to thwart the divine purpose. So Moses gave Hoshe'a an extended name, adding the name of God, *Yeho* to his name. His new name meant, 'May God save you – *Yeho-shua* – from the mischievous conspiracy of the other spies'.

Now, it is quite common practice for anyone called Joshua to have their friends shorten it to Josh. This is quite ironic when we consider that it was that short biblical name *Hoshe'a* – Josh – that was subsequently lengthened into *Yehoshua* – Joshua – and that now it is being shortened once again, by friends, to its original length!

But we should never forget the circumstances under which Hoshe'a's original name was lengthened into Yehoshua, that is, as a caution to a great man not to be influenced by the unworthy people around him.

Life is a minefield, and friends are very important. Indeed, in one of our earliest daily prayers we ask God – *V'harchikeinu mei'adam ra umeichaver ra* – 'To keep us far from bad people and bad friends.'

Generally we can measure people by the sort of company they keep and the people they choose as friends. If one leads the sort of life that is constructive, prayerful and charitable, the bad friends will soon lose interest and leave, and one will be left with the right type of friends.

And that caution is all contained in the expanded name Yehoshua, 'May God save you' – from the wrong type of friend.

CHAPTER FORTY-TWO

Korach:
The wisdom of women

We may not be surprised to learn that somewhere, well in the background of the bitter dispute between Moses and Korach, there was an *eishet chayil*, a woman of strength, who, although not referred to in the text, is praised in our oral, Midrashic tradition.

Among the main supporters of Korach listed at the beginning of today's sidrah were Datan and Aviram, 250 princes of Israel and another leader whose name is given as On ben Pelet, who hailed from the tribe of Reuven, not from Korach's Levite tribe.

At the end of the episode, when the rebels are defeated and about to meet their doom, God tells Moses to keep his distance from 'the group led by Korach, Datan and Aviram'. Surprisingly, God omits mention of the other rebel, On ben Pelet from the tribe of Reuven.

The rabbis explain this omission by telling us that, on the advice of his wise wife, his *eishet chayil*, On abandoned his support of the rebellion. His wife reasoned with him as follows: 'Whatever happens, you are the loser. If Moses wins, you remain subject to his authority, and if Korach wins, all the authority will be shared out to the members of his own tribe of Levi. Either way, you end up with nothing. Keep out of it, On', she advised, 'it's not your battle!' He listened to his wife, and he was saved.

Now, although there is a masculine equivalent of Bat Mitzvah, it is not surprising that there is no masculine equivalent of the term *Bat chayil* or *Eishet chayil*, 'woman of (moral) strength'. We do have a term *ish chayil* or *gibbor chayil*, but that has the exclusive sense of 'warrior'. Men give priority to their physical strength, their prowess at making war. When it comes to moral strength and practical wisdom, however, women are clearly the superior sex whose perceptions are generally far more accurate and mature.

This is the message of that tradition regarding the wife of On ben Pelet. It calls out to women to be a moderating influence on their husbands, especially if the latter happen to be impetuous, argumentative or thoughtless. Judaism has always recognized which of the sexes has the greater moral strength. This quality is to be prized, nurtured and developed.

CHAPTER FORTY-THREE

Chukat:
The relative value of mitzvot

We read in Ethics of the Fathers: 'Be as particular over a light mitzvah as over a weighty mitzvah, for you do not know the reward that is assigned for each mitzvah' (2: 1).

This assessment of the mitzvot has to be accurate, for, had God wanted the Torah's laws to be regarded as shares in a Stock Exchange index, from which one chooses the ones that appear to be the best investment, yielding the biggest returns, then God would certainly have provided a graduated scheme of mitzvot, indicating which are 'light' and which 'weighty', and possibly how may credits one might expect from the individual mitzvot in each of those categories.

But the Torah was not intended to be a 'lucky dip'. We are meant to strive to observe as many of its mitzvot as we can. And the very fact that we do not know the respective reward that each mitzvah brings actually helps us to view them all as 'equal in importance'.

But that opening quotation is not totally consistent, for there are at least two mitzvot that we are entitled to assess as truly 'weighty'. These are the commands regarding honouring parents and shooing away a mother bird so that she is not pained by the sight of her nest being rifled. In both cases the Torah discloses the reward that can be expected for their observance. For honouring parents: 'that your days may be long upon the land that the Lord thy God gives to you' (Exodus 20: 12); for shooing away the mother bird: 'that it may go well for you and you may prolong your days' (Deuteronomy 22: 7). We may confidently assume, therefore, that those two are indeed such 'weighty' mitzvot, offering such special rewards, that the Torah departed from its usual principle of withholding any mention of reward when formulating a mitzvah.

In the case of the mitzvah of honouring parents we can go further, and even place a monetary value upon it, albeit that this might well fluctuate depending on the market price. By this we do not mean the market price of the mitzvah, but of the *parah adumah*, the red calf, mentioned in our sidrah.

Now this will sound extremely mystifying until we acquaint ourselves with a fascinating story that the Midrash (*Devarim Rabba* 1: 14) relates about a jeweller called Dama ben Netina of Ashkelon whose reverence for his parents was absolutely unrivalled. It is related that his mother was of unstable mind, and she would enter his room while he was meeting with important colleagues and would slap his face. Dama never reacted with anger, or even displeasure, but would simply say, in a soft voice, 'Let that suffice, mother dear!'

But it is the next example of his respect for his father that is especially enlightening in relation to our subject of the monetary reward for that particular mitzvah of honouring parents. The Midrash relates that some sages came to Ashkelon to buy from Dama a replacement for one of the very precious gems that had fallen out of the High Priest's breastplate and was lost. The sages agreed a price of 1,000 gold pieces for the stone.

Dama then went to retrieve the key to the safe which his father always kept in a strong box in his bedroom. When he entered, he saw that his father was fast asleep with his legs resting upon the box. Dama would not disturb his father and he returned empty-handed. When the sages saw that he had returned without it, they immediately called out, 'Make it ten thousand gold pieces'. Dama replied: 'Far be it from me to make a profit out of the mitzvah of honouring my father. I will take only the thousand that we had agreed.'

The Midrash continues that God rewarded Dama for his zeal for that mitzvah, and during that very year his cow bore a *parah* adumah, a totally red calf, which he sold to the Temple authorities for more than 10,000 gold pieces. We may thus calculate that the monetary value of a mitzvah such as honouring parents equates to the market value of a *parah adumah* at any given time.

The birth of a *parah adumah* was so rare that, according to R. Meir (*Mishnah Parah* 3: 5), only seven such calves were ever found, and prepared for the special ritual of purification. One was born in the period of Moses, one in that of Ezra, and the other five during the 500 years from Ezra until the destruction of the Temple. One can imagine that the owner of such a perfectly red, flawless animal could demand whatever price he wanted. Possession of it by the Temple priests meant that they could resume the ritual of purifying those who had become impure through contact with the dead, and who had previously to keep away from visiting the Temple or coming into contact with sacred objects.

What is the lesson to be derived from all this? First and foremost the paramount importance of those two mitzvot: honouring parents and showing consideration for the feelings even of a mother bird. We can see the connection between those two mitzvot, since both involve the quality of concern and consideration, for man as well as for animals. Judaism believes that we cannot detach the two levels of concern. We must care for all God's creatures, great and small. That is not to say that we may not use birds and animals for food consumption. God has told us that that is acceptable, just as He prescribed the slaughter of animals for sacrifice. But when it comes to unnecessary and unproductive infliction of pain or suffering, then there can be no excuse for any cruelty or lack of consideration.

This is why Judaism would certainly be opposed to blood sports, and would welcome the ban against hunting that was recently introduced in Great Britain. However, it would support experimentation on animals if the results meant a breakthrough in our ability to cure life-threatening human diseases. Human life is, after all, paramount. And Judaism would be horrified at the 'animal rights' activists who think nothing of threatening, assaulting and endangering the lives of people involved in medical experimentation on animals. According to their distorted sense of priorities, animals are shown greater concern than humans.

There is so much here for our young adults to reflect upon: the importance of a total commitment to all mitzvot whether they appear 'light' or 'weighty'; the paramount importance of the mitzvah of honouring parents; the unexpected material rewards that God sometimes bestows for devotion to a mitzvah; the necessity to cultivate sensitivity, care and concern in our relationship with others; not to inflict unnecessary pain on animals, and to regard human life – and feelings – as being at the summit of our priorities.

CHAPTER FORTY-FOUR

Balak:
Let Bilaam be your guide!

This sidrah describes how the wicked king of Moab, Balak, hired a magician called Bilaam to curse Israel and destroy her. Our rabbis believe, however, that Bilaam was far more than a mere magician or caster of evil spells. They actually credit him with having been a distinguished prophet, a guide and counsellor to the heathen nations. The rabbis even seem to have gone overboard with their praise of his powers, claiming that 'in the same way that Moses was the chief of all the prophets of Israel, so Bilaam was the most distinguished counsellor and guide to the other nations' (Sifrei sec. 357). How do we explain this astonishing assessment and praise?

I suggest that the explanation lies in four remarkable statements that Bilaam makes when, under pressure from God, he spells out to King Balak why he cannot fulfil his mission to curse Israel (see Numbers 22: 18, 38; 23: 26; 24: 13). On the very first occasion he tells the king: 'If King Balak were to give me his palace full of silver and gold, I could not transgress the word of the Lord, my God.'

It is astonishing that that non-believer is suddenly filled with a spirit of truth to the extent that he has a revelation that the God of Israel is the supreme God, and that he simply cannot defy Him in any way. More than that, if we look up the other three passages we find that, on each occasion, Bilaam refers to Israel's God as either *Adonai* or *Elohim*, or, in the first instance, *Adonai Elohai*, 'The Lord my God.' In other words, he fully accepts upon himself the sovereignty of Israel's God, to the extent that he feels totally bound by whatever God desires of him. That surely goes a long way to explaining why the Talmudic sages elevated Bilaam to the status of a prophet, albeit to the other nations.

The rather unexpected message that this sidrah offers young adults is to follow Bilaam and to make his approach their own. They could do little better than paraphrase his words: 'If anyone were to offer me the greatest reward or inducement, I could not reject the word of the Lord, my God' (Numbers 22: 18).

There will certainly be those who will attempt to persuade young people to reject some of the cherished teachings of Judaism, or the moral and ethical standards that it sets. If ever that happens, they should think back to this sidrah and reflect on how even the non-believing magician, Bilaam, realized that God's word must be obeyed if we want peace of mind, joy and blessing in life. If Bilaam eventually realized that, should not we?

CHAPTER FORTY-FIVE

Pinchas:
Moses and the JWTK

The sidrah Pinchas presents a picture of two contrasting types of leader. On a number of occasions in his ministry Moses displayed firm and uncompromising leadership. One thinks instinctively of when he slew the Egyptian taskmaster and then rebuked the Israelite bully, and of the courage he displayed in his dealings with Pharaoh. Yet there were more occasions during his forty-year ministry when he seemed to display fear, timidity and a lack of belief in his own leadership ability.

This was demonstrated initially when he rejected God's summons to him to lead Israel, offering the lame excuse that *lo ish devarim anochi*, 'I am not an orator' (Exodus 4: 10). He then added, *shelach na b'yad tishlach*, 'Send someone else, please!' (4: 13) A little later, when his intervention on behalf of Israel became counterproductive, and their brick-making burden was intensified, Moses says to God, *Lamah harei'ota la'am ha-zeh*, 'Why have you done evil to this people? Why have you sent me?' (5: 22) Again, when the people had no water, at Rephidim, and bitterly complained against him, Moses' response was to turn away in fear and to cry out to God, *Od me'at uskaluni*, 'Help, they'll soon be stoning me!' (17: 2) This was hardly the level of leadership expected from one who, on a regular basis, saw God 'face to face'.

In the previous sidrah the Israelites displayed such an absence of fear of God or loyalty to Moses that they committed wholesale immorality with the Moabite women in the context of acts of idolatrous worship. Zimri, a prince of Israel, dragged a Midianite girl into the Israelite camp – which God had commanded should retain a strict level of holiness – and had sex with her in public.

There was a hush in the camp. The eyes of every Israelite were fixed on their leader, Moses. Could he possibly tolerate that behaviour in Israel, or would he now take swift action and make an example of the perpetrators, just as he had done years earlier when the Israelites danced around the Golden Calf?

Time seemed to stand still. No one moved. Moses stood as if rooted to the spot, speechless, and, as we have observed, not for the first time. It was clear that he was petrified into inaction. Without a divine voice prompting him, he was at a loss to know how to act. Was this the moment when all those spiritually and morally demanding laws, that reverberated around Sinai and that were etched into Tablets of Stone, were to be exposed as unattainable and unpunishable? Was Israel no holier than the surrounding nations? Did its Torah have no impact on their moral behaviour?

Suddenly there was a stir. The ranks of the bystanders parted, and a familiar figure stepped forward. It was Pinchas, son of Eleazar and grandson of Aaron. He looked at Moses for approbation, but received not a flicker of a reaction. So he seized a spear and ran it through the bodies of the two immoral idolators.

Two opposing reactions. Two paradigms of leadership in a time of crisis. Moses, the dreamer, the man whose hatred of violence was so profound that he was prepared to tolerate any situation in the hope that it would be resolved by faith and reliance on God rather than by physical retribution. Pinchas, on the other hand, who loved peace no less, but who knew that not all problems just go away of their own accord, and that a weak response to a violent or immoral situation is a recipe for disaster and national disintegration. Pinchas's moral zealotry was what was required at that moment, to save the nation and the moral and spiritual heritage to which it was committed.

The Talmud describes the total breakdown of moral courage in our leaders that can be expected in the period prior to the coming of the Messiah. It states p'nei ha-dor kifnei ha-kelev, 'the leaders of that generation will adopt the pose of a dog!' (Sota 49b) The Chafetz Chayim explains that a dog usually runs in front of its master, giving the impression that he is determining the way the master will go, but, in reality, it is the master who determines direction, and the dog will regularly look back to see where his master wants to walk. A leader who keeps looking back, like a dog, to see where the people want to go, is no leader. Moses had clearly reached the stage in his life when it was time for someone more decisive, courageous and forward-looking to take over the reins of leadership.

Yehudah Avner, a former Israeli ambassador to Great Britain, once described a confrontation in the King David Hotel in Jerusalem between the then newly elected Prime Minister, Menachem Begin and the great Oxford philosopher, Sir Isaiah Berlin. Begin, we recall, was the leader of the Jewish underground movement in Palestine, the Irgun, which had perpetrated acts of terror against the British Mandatory government of Palestine in 1944 in an attempt to get the British to leave the country so that a Jewish state could be founded. Sir Isaiah, by contrast, regarded the resorting to violence, no matter how noble the cause, as morally reprehensible.

Well, in that year of 1977 Menachem Begin had just been elected Prime Minister of Israel, and was in the King David Hotel for a victory celebration. The prime minister's party was waiting for a lift to an upper floor. The lift doors opened, and there was Sir Isaiah Berlin. 'Hello, Sir Isaiah, welcome to Israel', said Begin, extending his hand. The great pacifist philosopher looked at the extended hand, turned to the side and walked away.

When they got upstairs to their reception, Begin looked upset. His wife tried to calm him, saying, 'For thirty years you've had so many people turning their backs on you, and suddenly you're surprised that some still do. Sit down. Relax. Try one of these pastries.'

'Sir Isaiah has, of course, an extraordinary mind', granted Begin, seating himself on a couch and inviting his guests to join him. 'As a philosopher he's a genuine original thinker. But as a Zionist he's a JWTK.'

'A what?' asked all those around him, in unison.

'A JWTK – a Jew with trembling knees', said Begin. And the people around him laughed knowingly.

It occurred to me when I read Yehudah Avner's piece that in this sidrah we have that same cleavage between two contrasting leadership attitudes: Pinchas foreshadows the Begin approach, where if your enemy only understands, respects and will capitulate to, force, then force is justified. Moses, at that stage in his career at least, preferred the quiet life, the resolution of problems by negotiation, by making concessions, by appealing to the better nature of one's enemy. Moses, at that moment, abandoned decisive leadership and adopted the pose of the dog who only appears to be leading, but is in fact following. Moses, at that moment was a JWTK, 'a Jew with trembling knees'. And hence God rewarded Pinchas with the brit shalom, 'the covenant of peace'. Because peace cannot always be attained by peaceful means.

This sidrah's message is to remember Pinchas, and, like him, never to be a JWTK. It is to be proud of our Jewishness, zealous in studying it, observing it, promoting and defending it. It is to set our heart on becoming leaders of our community and our people, leaders with a stout heart, a clear mind, and knees that do not tremble however tense the situation and however difficult the challenge.

CHAPTER FORTY-SIX

Mattot:
A shared future?

The Talmud has an overriding principle, expressed as *Kol Yisrael areivim zeh lazeh*, 'All Jews are responsible one for the other' (Shevuot 39a). It is a beautiful principle, defining our relationship to fellow Jews as that of family, with all the duties of care and responsibility that family imposes, or should impose. The English idiom, 'Blood is thicker than water', is a mere affirmation of the existence of certain family ties, but it falls short of describing those ties in terms of 'responsibility'.

Abraham was the personification of the Torah's ethical principles, and the fact that he felt a duty of care towards his wider family underlies his immediate decision to go to war in order to rescue his estranged nephew, Lot, who was seized in the course of a major war involving nine Middle Eastern states (see Genesis ch. 14). It is that sense of concerned kinship that the Talmud uses to define the relationship that should bind one Jew to the next. The Sidrah Mattot describes an attempt by two-and-a-half tribes of Israel to evade that particular responsibility toward their brethren of the other tribes.

As the Israelites were approaching the Promised Land, the tribes of Reuven, Gad and half the tribe of Menasseh saw that their large herds were thriving on the lush pasturage of the land they travelled through on the east bank of the River Jordan. They approached Moses with a request: 'If we have found favour in your sight, let this land be given to your servants as a heritage. Do not make us pass over the Jordan' (Numbers 32: 5).

In other words, they were asking permission to separate from their brethren and to stay exactly where they were, playing no further part in whatever struggles lay ahead for the rest of Israel. They knew full well that their brethren were going to encounter armed resistance from the existing Canaanite tribes, since the men that Moses had sent to spy out the land had already returned with a report referring to warlike and giant-like inhabitants. The two-and-a-half tribes must have known that their support was indispensable to Israel if they were to succeed in the conquest of the land. And yet they proceeded to make that outrageous request!

Moses, not surprisingly, reacted sharply to their words: 'Shall your brothers go out to battle while you stay here? Why are you causing the hearts of the Israelites to have misgivings about being able to enter the land that the Lord has given to them?' (32: 6–7)

Moses then proceeded to equate their irresponsible request with the action of the spies whose false report had injected fear, despair and lack of faith into the hearts of the nation. This response might seem, at face value, to be rather an over-reaction on Moses' part, bearing in mind that the spies were in truth guilty of misleading the nation whereas the two-and-a-half tribes had merely put in a thoughtless request.

There is clearly much to learn from Moses' reaction, primarily that although it is true that 'actions speak louder than words', yet words, even those that may appear harmless, can also send clear and negative messages. The rabbis have a maxim, *Dai lechakima bi-remizah*, 'A wise man needs no more than a hint'. He readily infers the implication of what is said to him; he does not require it to be spelt out fully. The rest of the nation understood clearly the full implication of those tribes' request to Moses. Without the support of that fifth of the Israelites – and the tribe of Gad constituted a particularly strong fighting force (see Deuteronomy 33: 20) – the rest of the nation would have immediately feared that their chances of successfully conquering the land were seriously reduced. Furthermore, the idea that any pasturage could be superior to that awaiting them in Canaan would also have seriously reduced in their eyes the truth of God's promise that they were coming into a most fertile land, 'flowing with milk and honey'.

Thus, even the mere request of the two-and-a-half tribes was a body-blow to Moses' public relations exercise of encouraging the nation to go forward into conquest with courage, hope and faith.

This entire episode hinges on the issue of the unity of the Jewish people and the place of the land of Israel in the hearts of all Jews. It spells out in no uncertain terms the sense of responsibility that those who choose, for whatever reason or none, to live outside Israel, should nevertheless feel towards their brothers and sisters who are citizens of the state.

It is the latter who have been building up, defending and sacrificing their lives to ensure that we have a land to call our own, to take pride in, and to return to either out of love or out of necessity if the going gets tough for Jews in the Diaspora. It is vital for every Jew to feel that Israel is his or her homeland whether or not they have as yet chosen to live there. This has always been the Diaspora's attitude whenever Israel was threatened by her enemies. When the state of Israel was proclaimed in 1948, and five Arab armies declared war on it, Jews from all over the world made their way there to enlist in the newly formed Israeli army. Notwithstanding the difficult economic conditions in the period following Israel's victory in that 'War of Independence', her population practically doubled in the following three years, from 665,000 in May 1948 to about 1,330,000 in 1951, to over 1,600,000 by May 1952. It was the youth that spearheaded that expansion in population and regeneration of the country.

I can also personally recall the rallies held in London at the outbreak of the 'The Six Days War' (1967), 'The Yom Kippur War' (1973), and, more recently, the war against Hizbollah in Lebanon (2006), when people donated money to the war effort, literally 'until it hurt'. I vividly recall a public meeting at my synagogue in 1967 where the women spontaneously took off their precious and expensive engagement rings and donated them to the cause. That was an eloquent measure of the sense of unity that binds us to Medinat Yisrael, and an acknowledgment of the fact that when Israel is in danger, so are we.

We must all work towards intensifying that relationship and sense of identification, through regular visits, study trips, earnest attempts to master the language and a wish to make *aliyah* and be part of that great and miraculous enterprise. Israel is a land of opportunity, at the cutting edge of scientific and medical research, a country rich in spiritual vitality and artistic creativity of all kinds, a country of entrepreneurial inventiveness and industrial output. It is a country where young people thrive and where over 50 per cent of the country is under 30 years of age. It is a country of the present and the future, unlike so many countries in Europe which are so clearly in decline, having lost their vision, vitality and sense of mission.

Israel, the country of the future, calls out to young Jews the world over, 'Come home and be part of that future.' Well, how about it?

CHAPTER FORTY-SEVEN

Massei:
Women's rights in Judaism

In the previous sidrah we described Moses' condemnation of the tribes who requested to be allocated territory east of the Jordan, instead of joining their brethren in the Promised Land. Moses understandably construed that request as calculated to inject fear into the other tribes, as well as impugning the quality of the Land of Israel proper.

The sidrah Massei is intrinsically connected to the previous sidrah, Mattot, and indeed in most years these two sidrot are read as one. Their respective themes are similarly connected. Having described the two-and-a-half tribes' petition, Massei goes on to describe the various boundaries of the land that was left for the remaining tribes to occupy as their eternal possession. It also names the leaders, Eleazar and Joshua, and identifies the princes, one from each tribe, who were to oversee the division of the land to ensure that each tribe occupied its rightful possession and did not encroach upon the territory of a neighbouring tribe.

Massei also prescribes that there should be made available forty-eight cities, spread across the tribal lands, that were to be exclusively for priestly occupation, as well as six 'cities of refuge' – three on either side of the Jordan – to which someone who had killed another accidentally might flee to avoid the violent retribution of any near relative of the victim.

Staying with that theme of land division and inheritance, the sidrah describes the objection raised by one family from the line of Joseph to the decision made in Pinchas, that the five daughters of

Zelafchad could inherit their father's land in the absence of any male heir (Numbers 27: 1–11). The objection, that, if the girls were ever to marry members of other tribes, their own God-given tribal land would then automatically pass to their husbands' tribes and deplete their own, was upheld by Moses. He added a caveat, therefore, that the girls could only choose husbands from their own tribe.

There is a most profound lesson to be derived from that family's objection to the law of inheritance that God had promulgated. Interestingly, it was an objection on top of the previous objection of the girls themselves to a law that they regarded as discriminating against women.

Does that mean that God had overlooked that weakness in a law that He, himself, had made? Furthermore, surely God, who foresees the future, must have known that those girls would one day raise their objection to Moses. Why then did He not build into the law at the outset that piece of legislation covering a situation where there were no male heirs?

To answer this we have to go back three sidrot, and read the account of Moses' response to the girls' objection to the law of inheritance that excluded them. There we are told that, after hearing their petition, Moses was unable to give a judicial decision (see Numbers 27: 4). He either did not know the law, because God had not discussed that particular situation with him during Moses' stay on Mount Sinai, or, being human, he had forgotten what God had told him.

The rabbis offer both alternatives. One view is that God made Moses forget the law he had already been told. This was a punishment for Moses having, uncharacteristically, used rather boastful language when he addressed his newly appointed judges. He told them, 'Whatever is too difficult for you, you shall submit to me, and I shall hear it' (Deuteronomy 1: 17). To teach Moses a lesson in humility, God made him forget the law in the case of that major issue of female inheritance (Tal. Sanhedrin 8a). A second interpretation has it that God consciously held back from discussing this aspect of the law with Moses in order to confer special merit upon the daughters of Zelafchad, that they might initiate, through their petition, a piece of Torah legislation.

The lesson to be derived from the first interpretation is self-evident. Boastfulness is unacceptable. The book of Proverbs expresses this most succinctly: *Yehallelcha zar v'lo picha*, 'Let others praise you, but not your own mouth' (Proverbs 27: 2). (Interestingly, some suggest a different phrasing of the words of that maxim, namely, *Yehallelcha zar*, 'Let others praise you'; *velo*, 'And if they do not', then − *picha* − 'your own lips may do so'. This is the justification of praising one's own achievements, say, in a curriculum vitae. Obviously, if one does not list one's achievements in such a document, one will have no chance of securing the place or job one is hoping to obtain.) We live in an age of self-promotion, with publicity and public relations having developed into a vast industry. It is all the more difficult, therefore, for those attributes of modesty and humility to be integrated into one's character and personality as our tradition requires. As with most things in life: we must aim for a sense of balance and proportion.

The lesson to be derived from the second interpretation of Moses' inability to give a decision to the girls is that God cares for the rights of women. This is something that is overlooked in some Orthodox circles. Women not only have the right to economic security, but also to spiritual individuality. And this is why the present writer always supported the wish of some women in his community to have their own Women's Tefillah Group on a Shabbat morning. If we look back at the verse describing how Moses brought the daughters of Zelafchad's petition to God for a decision, we will see that our textual tradition prescribes the writing of an inordinately long final *nun* at the end of the word *mishpatan*, 'their petition' (Numbers 27: 5). We may view that *nun* as representing the initial letter of the word *nekevah*, meaning 'female', as a message that feminine rights must always be respected and promoted.

One final thought: when reference is made to those who objected to the fact that, if allowed to marry outside their own tribe, the daughters of Zelafchad would then be transferring their ancestral land to the tribes of their husbands, the Torah saw fit to provide the complete genealogy of the objectors, 'from the family of the sons of Gil'ad, son of Machir, son of Menasseh, of the families of the sons of Joseph' (Numbers 36: 1).

137

Is there not a huge irony here? After all, Joseph was the only son of Jacob who was privileged to have become the ancestor of two separate tribes, Ephraim and Menasseh. Direct descendants of Joseph should have been the very last ones, therefore, to have objected to any tribal land being redistributed!

The Torah does not spell out any overt criticism of those Josephite objectors, but it certainly hints at it. The proverb, 'those who live in glass houses shouldn't throw stones', or, as the Talmud puts it, 'those who have quenched their thirst at a well should not then throw a clod of earth into it', would seem to lie implicit within the Torah's having spelt out the full Josephite genealogy of the objectors!

When we consider, out of all the potential suitors from the 32,200 servicemen of their own tribe (see Numbers 2: 21), which husbands were provided for these five girls, namely their own first cousins, it certainly looks as if the 'family' objectors to their out-marriage had one mighty ulterior motive in wanting to narrow down (to themselves) the list of potential suitors!

PART FIVE

DEVARIM

CHAPTER FORTY-EIGHT

Devarim:
The importance of learning
from history

The entire book of Devarim is essentially one long speech by Moses to his people in the fortieth year of their desert wandering. Moses knew that, by divine command, he was not destined to enter the Promised Land, so he seized the rapidly closing window of opportunity to leave his people with a final message.

In it he surveys the past forty years of wandering and alludes to the setbacks they had suffered, punishments for the various demonstrations of faithlessness and rebellion on the part of the nation, particularly the acts of idolatry and immorality with neighbouring tribes. He also reflects on the tribulations that he had personally experienced as he had attempted to lead a stiff-necked people to their destiny. He warns them about the temptations awaiting them in Canaan, and he exhorts them to obey God's will if they are to retain their sovereignty and enjoy the fruits of the covenant that they signed together at Sinai. In addition, he highlights, in his own words, some of the principal laws that had previously been given at Sinai, and in some cases he exhorts Israel to be especially zealous in their observance. He ends his lengthy address by choosing his successor, Joshua, and with the composition of a special song of praise, Ha'azinu, and a final blessing to each of the tribes, contained in the final sidrah, V'zot ha-brachah.

There are several amazing aspects of this speech, notably its status, its orator, its oratory and its length.

By its status we mean that Moses' own words were elevated in sanctity to become an integral part of the Torah itself. Moses was, after all, a mere mortal, one whose haste caused him to forfeit his lifetime's dream of leading his people into the Promised Land. And yet that flawed individual – from God's perspective – is granted the supreme privilege of a shared authorship with God in the Torah to be bestowed upon the world. God wrote the first four books; Moses the fifth. And together they become the Torah. Moses' book-within-a-book, his unoriginal digest of God's previous books, is yet referred to as *Mishneh Torah*, 'the repetition of the Law', while the Greek-speaking Jews of the third century BCE translated that term as *Deuteronomion*, which means 'The Second Law', with its overtone of one that equals, if not surpasses, the first.

There is a most inspirational and challenging message here, for all ages. It is that we all have unique insights to contribute to the elucidation of Torah. We may not have the insights of a Moses, we may even be flawed in some respects – such as in the breadth and depth of our knowledge – but we still have the prerogative, if not the mission, to interpret Torah afresh, to extract our own distinctive message, according to our own perspectives and the experiences and emotions we bring to the text. That is precisely what Moses did. God gave the Torah from His perspective; but Moses, a mere mortal, was expected to reinterpret it afresh from his. The Torah does not necessarily stimulate within the minds of youth the same thoughts or emotions as it does for adults, neither will those respective age-profiles take away the same life-messages.

The second amazing facet of Moses' Devarim speech is its oratory and length. There is a great touch of irony in the fact that, Moses, who initially rejected God's summons to become the leader of Israel on the grounds that, *lo ish devarim anochi*, 'I am not a man of words' (Exodus 4: 10), ends his mission by becoming, precisely, *ish Devarim*, 'the man of the book of Devarim'. Similarly, of all the qualities and skills that Moses possessed, the very one that he so vehemently denied himself, that of orator, is the one most finely honed and demonstrated in the majestic style and rich language of the book he authored. For a man who began life with seriously restricted powers of oratory, is it not amazing that later in life he was able to hold the attention of an entire people with a speech the length of an entire book?

There is a message in this for the vast number of young people who, through lack of self-confidence, self-belief, motivation, encouragement by parents or teachers, or through lack of opportunity, fail to exploit their inner talents and skills and to rise to the heights that they might so well have scaled.

Moses left his hesitancy, his stammer, his self-doubts behind. He liberated himself from his own 'self', and became exclusively focused upon what he had to do for others. And in dedicating himself to others, he found himself. He shed his inhibitions and displayed to the full his powers, his strength of character, his natural talent and authority.

There are many other interesting aspects of this, the most personal of the five 'Books of Moses' – in the sense of it being Moses' own book. One obvious question relates to the value of the book. After all, if it is merely a re-statement of what is already chronicled in the rest of the Torah, a digest of the past forty years of the nation's wanderings, then who needs it? Certainly not the generation that experienced it!

We must not forget that the people of Moses' generation were condemned to die in the desert because of their lack of faith and their belief in the false report of the spies. Only the younger generation, under twenty at the time of that incident (see Numbers 14: 29), was destined to enter the Promised Land.

Moses' insistence on repeating the events of their immediate past history is most instructive. He was making the point that the lessons of history have to be taught and retaught to every new generation, because, however cataclysmic those events may have been, the young generation has little interest in them and even less to confront them. For them, they are history; and history has a surreal quality about it. It is not reality. It is 'his story', rather than mine. It describes a fate visited upon their parents' generation, in circumstances that were unrelated to their own 'modern' experience. But Moses insisted on retelling the younger generation the history of their parents' generation because he knew full well that they could, and they would, make exactly the same mistakes, ignoring the warning signs and experiencing the same setbacks and suffering.

Moses gave them the clear and timely message that the lessons of history, like human nature, do not change, that whoever does not study and learn from history's mistakes will be condemned to repeat them, and that, in an age of weapons of mass destruction, the punishment for ignoring history has the potential to be global, rather than regional.

We Jews have to be vocal on this matter. We have to demand vigilance and stiff penalties for those who foment anti-Semitism and racism. It was our high profile fight for the Soviet *refusniks* that embarrassed the Russian authorities and moved their cause high up on the list of international government and media priorities. We who know our history, and we who have suffered more than any other nation from its excesses, must not relax for a moment. We must agitate, lobby and fight for justice and survival. And that lobbying cannot start early enough – in schools and universities. Our enemies are lobbying there. Jewish youth have to prepare themselves to join the struggle.

Yigal Allon, a past deputy prime minister of Israel, related that when he learnt as a child that the Messiah has been sitting waiting for a few thousand years by the gates of Rome, disguised as a poor leper (Tal. Sanhedrin 98a), he asked his aged teacher what the Messiah was waiting for. The answer he received changed the course of his life:'

He was waiting for you!'

CHAPTER FORTY-NINE

Va'etchanan:
Freedom from parental control?

At the end of his life, in the last year of Israel's wandering in the desert, Moses addresses Israel and reviews all the events of the previous four decades. He also repeats the Ten Commandments that had been given to Israel shortly after they had left Egypt and which have contributed more to human development than any other document in history. At Sinai man was given a moral constitution in the form of guidelines for the establishment of a society wherein man would be duty-bound to respect his neighbour's life, rights and property. Without that revelation at Sinai, civilization could never have developed and the law of the jungle would have prevailed.

The Torah taught us – and, through us, the world – the meaning of discipline, of curbing our desires and passions, of accepting that there have to be restraints on our freedom of will, on how we may behave and what we can legitimately acquire, and that, no matter how desirable that which belongs to our neighbour may be, it is wrong for us to be envious and to contrive to secure it by force or subterfuge.

There was once a local newspaper that ran a competition to find out who was the most well-behaved, model and exemplary citizen among its readership. One of the replies was from a man who boasted, 'I do not smoke, drink, gamble or cheat on my wife, nor do I shirk any job I am given to do. I do not waste my time going to movies, clubs or restaurants. I am in bed every night on time, awake bright and early every morning, and regularly attend religious services.'

In conclusion the man made the following observation: 'I've behaved like this for the last ten years. But just you wait till next year when they let me out of this hole!'

There is a parallel here to the state of young adulthood. That man in prison behaved himself only because he had no choice. He implied, however, that once he had gained his freedom he would seize the opportunity to indulge to excess, to make up for all the things denied him for so long. Until Bar or Bat Mitzvah a child is totally under the control of its parents, and they are expected to discipline and lay down the law, certainly as regards social behaviour and moral and religious conduct.

From the age of Bar and Bat Mitzvah young people become responsible before God for their own actions, for what they do that is wrong, and for what they fail to do that is right and worthy. From that age, parental control in religious matters is relaxed. If parents have done their work of spiritual parenting properly, then the young person ought to be quite capable of making the right decisions in every situation of life. If they have trained their child in the ways of Judaism, we may assume that as a young adult he or she will already have the knowledge, pride and motivation to be observant and loyal to our heritage for the rest of their life.

CHAPTER FIFTY

Eikev:
Consideration for the disabled

In this section of Moses' lengthy farewell speech that constitutes the book of Devarim he recalls the time God told him to ascend Sinai a second time to receive a replacement set of tablets for the ones he smashed in anger when he saw the Israelites worshipping the Golden Calf (Deuteronomy 10: 1–6).

But we may well inquire as to what happened to the fragments of the first set of tablets that were scattered around the foot of Mount Sinai (see Exodus 32: 19)? Surely, once his anger had abated, Moses would never have treated them irreverently by leaving them behind on the ground! After all, inscribed on those stone fragments were letters of the Ten Commandments hewn out miraculously by the very hand of God!

The answer of the Rabbis was Luchot v'shivrei luchot munachin ba'aron, 'Both the replacement tablets and the broken fragments from the first tablets were placed side by side inside the Ark' (Tal. Berachot 8b). Thus, not only did Moses not abandon them on the ground, but he actually housed them in the identical place of honour occupied by the second, complete tablets.

But the sages, ever on the lookout for further profound moral lessons that may be inferred from every biblical occurrence, derived a most important teaching from the fact that 'the broken fragments' were also treated so reverently: 'From here we learn', they said, 'that we must show the greatest respect for a scholar who has forgotten his learning through dementia' (Tal. Menachot 99a).

This sensitive advice speaks directly to our modern age which, for all its shortcomings, can boast a heightened sense of concern for the disabled. Much has been done over the past fifty or so years towards lightening their burden and introducing legislation to make life, and especially mobility, easier for the physically and mentally handicapped. When I was a child, physical disability was accepted, since, in the aftermath of two world wars, there were many servicemen who returned minus limbs. Mental illness, on the other hand, had a particular stigma attached to it, and people with emotional stress were frequently banished to what were called 'lunatic asylums'. In an earlier age, people who displayed behavioural problems were suspected of being witches, and were either burned at the stake or incarcerated in jails for the rest of their lives.

These days we understand so much more about brain chemistry, and how the slightest imbalance in that area can cause uncontrollable physical reactions. We now know how emotional stress can manifest itself externally through mood swings, depression, migraine and skin eruptions. We understand so much more today about the complexity of human beings and the interrelationship of their mental and physical states. We are so much more tolerant and sympathetic today toward people with 'stress-related problems', since we realize that most of the world's population suffers in some measure, at any given time, from its effects, especially given the unprecedented stresses of modern living and the breakdown of family life.

When a scholar suffers from dementia or memory loss it is especially evident and sad, and the contrast between his former state of intellectual agility and instant recall and his current state of unresponsiveness is particularly acute. When a Torah sage falls victim to Alzheimers and can no longer even recite the *Shema*, or when a university professor can no longer even recognize his family, it is more than pitiful, not only for them but also for society which has been deprived of their further contribution. In a past age they were neglected and left to vegetate. Today they are cared for and stimulated to maximize whatever of their potential still remains.

It should be a source of pride to us that our sages already

understood the problem and empathized with the sufferers some 2,000 years ago. The fact that both the complete and the fractured tablets were given the same place of honour in the Sanctuary's Ark was a powerful message to Jewish society to extend sympathy and a helping hand to all who were 'broken' in body or spirit.

There is a special challenge here for young adults, which they can fulfil by befriending the disabled, helping with programmes organized for them or raising funds for their support and rehabilitation. In addition they can remember how vulnerable all human beings are and how easily and suddenly our lives can be tragically overturned. This, in turn, should motivate them to be grateful to God for each and every day of good health that they enjoy. That is surely the greatest blessing of all.

CHAPTER FIFTY-ONE

Eikev:
Picking and choosing mitzvot

This sidrah contains a summons to Israel which is particularly relevant to young adults, namely to keep all the mitzvot. It states: *Kol ha-mitzvah* — 'Every commandment which I command you this day, you shall observe and do' (Deuteronomy 8: 1). At least, that is the usual translation.

But some Hebrew words have more than one meaning, or they may refer to more than one aspect of the same idea. This is the case with the word *kol*. In most cases *kol* means 'every', as in the phrase we just quoted, *Kol ha-mitzvah*, 'every commandment'. As such, it represents a challenge to us to keep every single mitzvah and not to neglect a single one.

But *kol* can also mean 'the whole', 'the entirety', as in the call of the *Shema*, to love the Lord our God — *bechol levavcha uv'chol nafshe'cha uv'chol m'odecha* — 'with our entire heart, our entire soul and our entire might'.

The Midrash explains that the summons in our sidrah to keep *kol ha-mitzvah*, is intended in both senses of *kol*. Not only must we strive to keep each and every commandment, but also to observe each one in its entirety, to study it closely and fully in order to be able to fulfil it to the letter.

It is for this reason that if someone embarks upon a mitzvah and then leaves it to someone else to complete, it is credited to the spiritual account of the one who actually completes it. An example of this is found in the verse in Joshua (24: 23) which refers to 'the bones of Joseph which the *Children of Israel* brought up from

Egypt' [and carried with them for burial in the Promised Land]. If we read the book of Shemot (Exodus 13: 19), however, we are told that it was Moses who made it his personal mitzvah to carry the coffin of Joseph through the desert. So why does the book of Joshua credit that mitzvah to the Children of Israel, and not to Moses? The answer is that although Moses occupied himself with that worthy mitzvah throughout the desert, nevertheless, because he was prevented from entering Israel, and had to hand over the completion of that task to others, that mitzvah accrued to their credit. Moses performed the mitzvah, but not *kol ha-mitzvah*, 'the entirety of the mitzvah'.

There are many Jews who mistakenly regard the Torah as a smorgasbord, from which they can pick and choose however much or little they desire to observe. Some will keep their home strictly kasher but will eat anything available when out. Some will light candles, and eat their Friday night or festival eve meal at home in the traditional manner, but then watch television or go to outside entertainment as if it were any ordinary night, rather than a holy time. Some will go to shul in the morning, but to a football match in the afternoon.

This is the message of the phrase *kol ha-mitzvah*. Not only must we keep *all* the mitzvot we possibly can, but we must also try to fulfil them in the other sense of *kol*, namely in their entirety, without compromise. We should do so with enthusiasm, out of conviction, and on the basis of knowledge. We should not pick and choose. We should also see the mitzvah through, and earn the reward and the sense of pride and fulfilment from so doing.

CHAPTER FIFTY-TWO

Re'ei:
Making the right choices

The sidrah Re'ei opens with the theme of 'choice': *Re'eh anochi notein lifneichem hayom berachah uklalah*, 'Behold I am setting before you today a [way to acquire] blessing or a curse'. Commentators ask why the verb appears in the form *notein*, the present continuous tense, 'I am setting before you,' instead of, as expected, the past tense, *natati*, 'I have set before you'.

The great Vilna Gaon (1720–97) explained that the Torah employs the present continuous tense in order to teach us that the choice between good and evil that God gave Israel was not a one-off challenge, but rather a dilemma that is truly 'continuous', that faces us every single day of our lives, as we confront temptations in every area of our activity. Every day we read in the papers or hear on the news of famous, wealthy and influential people making the wrong choices, risking their reputations and livelihood, and thinking that they will not be found out. And all for some temporary advantage or benefit.

We hear of sportsmen and women taking drugs to enhance their performance, of cricketers taking bribes to fix matches, of politicians being paid to raise questions in parliament in order to benefit a specific interest-group, of government ministers awarding contracts to particular firms in return for money or trips abroad. We hear of people cheating in exams or pretending to possess qualifications that they have not acquired. At every turn in life we are beset by the need to choose between doing good with no personal advantage or succumbing to wrongdoing that offers personal gain.

Those temptations are so great that Hillel advised, *Al ta'amin b'atzmecha ad yom motcha*, 'Do not believe in yourself – in your capacity to resist – until your last day on earth' (*Pirkei Avot* 2: 5).

But that is precisely what makes life such a challenge. And that is what makes Jewish values so important, urgent and rewarding. Without our Torah, without the *dos* and *don'ts*, we would all be sucked into the whirlpool of temptation and sin. And in such an environment no one would be safe from violence and fraud. There would be no sense of holiness, of righteousness, of goodness and charitableness, no conscience and no sense of duty and integrity. Life would be a jungle, and we would all be at the mercy of forces and passions that we could not control or protect ourselves against.

So it is well worth remembering Vilna Gaon's observation on the present continuous tense of the verb *notein*, namely that every single day of our life *continuous* choices have to be made between right and wrong, blessing and curse, actions that will elicit praise and those that will inevitably incur censure. The corollary is that every day of our life we are given the opportunity of responding to God's will and amassing an abundance of blessing when we make the right and noble choices.

CHAPTER FIFTY-THREE

Shoftim:
Valuing every human being

The sidrah Shoftim speaks of the equality of all mankind and the obligation to administer justice and charitableness to all men without any trace of partiality. To that end, it commanded the king to carry with him at all times a miniature Torah scroll and to read it every day of his life so that he might be constantly reminded of his duties and responsibilities to God and to his fellow man.

The Torah adds another objective of that exercise, namely, *levilti rum levavo mei'echav*, 'that his heart be not exalted over his brethren'(Deuteronomy 17: 20). The king had to remember constantly that he was also subject to the same law as his subjects. He may have enjoyed greater privileges than them, but he also had greater responsibilities. Indeed, it was his special task to ensure that they enjoyed prosperity, protection and peace. He had to view himself as no more special in the eyes of God than any of his citizens.

We are all created 'in the image of God', and in that respect a king or queen is truly no more special than a commoner. Often it is the ordinary folk around us who enrich our lives far more than the so-called rich and famous. This was illustrated by a piece that I read some time ago, written by Charles Schultz, the creator of the 'Peanuts' comic strip. He made his point by asking his readers to respond to a quiz. In the first section he asked questions like: name six people who have won the Nobel or Pulitzer prize; the five wealthiest people in the world; last year's Academy Award winner for best actor; man of the match of the first test match in the current Ashes series; and winner of the men's final at Wimbledon in 2001.

Most of his readers made a very poor showing. In truth, we hardly remember the headline makers of yesterday, however talented or brilliant they may have been. The applause dies down and the achievements are forgotten by most of us.

He then asked them to respond to another quiz, wherein he asked such questions as: list two teachers who made the greatest impression on you throughout your school life; name two friends who helped you through a difficult time in your youth; name someone who became a role model for you in your professional or business life, opening your eyes to ways of doing things that greatly improved your own performance and led to greater achievement; and name a few people who made you feel particularly special.

This quiz found most people gaining full marks. The lesson was clearly that the people who make a difference in our lives are not the most famous, the ones with the most money or the most awards. They are the ones who care, the ones who see potential in others and assist them to nurture it, the ones who view all men as equals, as precious, as created in the image of God.

Hinnei mah tov umma na'im, shevet achim gam yachad – 'See how good and beautiful it is when brethren dwell together.'

CHAPTER FIFTY-FOUR

Ki Teitzei:
Ever on the move

With the end of the Torah in view there is a simple thought to be derived from the names of the remaining sidrot of the Torah. The first thing to notice is that they all involve 'motion'. *Ki Teitzei*, means, 'When you go out.' Next week's sidrah is *Ki Tavo*, 'when you come in,' which is followed by *Nitzavim*, meaning 'standing up', which is, in turn, followed by *Vayeilech*, 'And he went.' Then comes *Ha'azinu*, 'listening' – which also involves the movement of sound waves being transmitted to our ears. And the final sidrah of the Torah is *V'zot habrachah*, 'and this is the blessing that Moses gave', with the opening words of that blessing also alluding to motion: *Adonai MiSinai ba*, 'God came from Sinai'.

It is as if the Torah is emphasizing that a person should never stand still and rest on his or her laurels, or on what they have learnt in Hebrew classes, school, university, yeshivah or seminary. In religious life there are always greater and greater challenges to accept, higher peaks to scale and deeper levels of learning to plumb. We believe that if one does not move forward, one goes backward. And this underlies the English term for 'improvement of one's standard or performance'. We call it 'progress', which is derived from two Latin words meaning 'to move forward'. And this message is also conveyed by the Hebrew term for Jewish law, which is *halachah*, from the verb *halach*, 'to walk' – 'to keep moving forward'.

We Jews have always been 'on the move', both physically and intellectually. We have never rested on our laurels, content with the achievements we have notched up. We have always struggled to push forward the frontiers of knowledge and achievement, to travel to the most distant of places in search of new opportunities. This is why Jews were always to be found, all over the globe, creating vibrant new communities.

Frequently such migrations were forced upon us as we were exiled from one host country and forced to seek a home and protection in another. This is how we carried our Torah and its values across the world and became a 'light unto the nations'.

We view this mission as reflected in the names of the final sidrot of the Torah which, as we have shown, all bear that nuance of motion, mobility, progress and vitality. Not surprisingly the Torah regularly employs that same imagery when it urges us to 'walk in its ways' – constantly, confidently and proudly.

CHAPTER FIFTY-FIVE

Ki Tavo:
Youth, self-restraint and loyalty to Israel

The sidrah Ki Tavo refers to the duty of the ancient Israelite farmer to bring a gift of the first fruits and cereals of his harvest to the Temple. An act of great self-restraint and discipline was involved in this. The farmer had invested a goodly amount of his money, time and effort into producing his harvest. This involved purchasing seed, fertilizer, hiring help, equipment, sowing, irrigating, hoeing, weeding, tending, reaping, sorting, boxing and labelling. He would have to wait at least six months before his fields could be harvested, the produce marketed, and some profit enjoyed.

Imagine his great excitement when that moment arrived. Imagine his impatience to taste and to market the fruit of his labours! And yet, just at that moment, the Torah steps in and says,

> Hold it! You cannot proceed to enjoy the season's luscious produce just yet, for there is still one essential act to be done. That is to visit the Temple with a sample of that produce and there to thank God for the gifts of that land.
>
> The one thing the Jew must not do is take for granted the gift of the Land of Israel. And this is as true today as it was when our ancestors lived in that land in Temple times, some three thousand years ago. Hence the continued relevance of the second blessing of the Grace After Meals which praises God for the gifts of *eretz chemdah tovah urchavah*, 'a most desirable, goodly and spacious land'.

Interestingly, when the farmer eventually brought his first fruits to the Temple, the declaration he made drew attention to the fact that there was a lengthy period that his ancestors had to wait – more patiently than him – before they could enjoy that special gift of a land of their own. The farmer placed his gifts at the side of the altar and pronounced, *Arami oved avi*, 'My father [Jacob] was a wandering Aramean', who went down to Egypt, and whose offspring had to stay in that land of bondage for hundreds of years until, by God's grace, they were redeemed and brought to the Promised Land.

Even more than those ancient farmers, we have waited patiently for some two thousand years to repossess and enjoy that land. Our post-Holocaust generation knows full well that that land is our nation's sole refuge, our means of identity, of religious and cultural expression and our primary source of pride and national self-respect.

We can appreciate therefore why it was that the ancient Israelite farmer could not exploit that land as if it were exclusively his own, as if it were mere soil, rather than soul: a nation's spiritual and national home. And that is why he had first to offer a gift of thanksgiving and gratitude to the God of Israel who gave His people that land as a sign of the covenant between them.

Young adulthood is also a long-awaited moment of harvest when the seeds of all the parental love, care, education and religious training begin to bear fruit, and the young person may be credited with having the maturity to plan his or her own future and determine their independent destiny.

Many teenagers, however, launch themselves immediately into the enjoyment of the fruits of life and the pleasures of adulthood. Many indulge in the sampling of 'forbidden fruit', and end up doing incalculable physical and moral harm to themselves.

So the first message to be derived from the context of the first fruits is to remember how the Israelite farmer had to exercise self-discipline, and wait until the moment was right for him to enjoy what was available to him. It says to young people,

> Enjoy your youth. It is a most wonderful stage of life. Be assured, however, that it passes so very quickly, and before long you will be burdened with exams to determine your

place at university, possibly with heavy student debt, with extra responsibilities, and the pressure of finding a job in a competitive market. So do not be desperate to be an adult before your time. Remember that the ancient farmer had first to bring those fruits to the Temple. And you can learn a lesson for life from that. If ever you are unsure about whether to indulge in one of life's adult fruits, just imagine yourself standing in the Temple or synagogue, and announcing that intention to the congregation. If you would be embarrassed to do so, then you can be sure you are on the wrong track!

The second message is to remember the content of the farmer's *Arami oved avi* declaration, which is quoted in the Pesach Haggadah. It is a profound expression of appreciation for the gift of Israel, the land of our ancestors, after years of exile and oppression, and a call especially to our own young people to remain loyal to that age-old dream of ours, now a reality, of having a land of our own. It is also a caution for them to note how beset we still are by terrorists, hostile nations, politicians and leaders who still begrudge us that land and who are determined to deny our historical claim to it and to take it away from us by force.

Israel needs the first fruits of every young man and woman, by way of their support, their loyalty, their determination to uphold her cause, to spend time there, perhaps at a yeshivah or seminary, if not ultimately to live there and help the Jewish dream come true when *veshavu vanim ligvulam*, 'our young people will return to their rightful borders'.

CHAPTER FIFTY-SIX

Nitzavim:
The Israelite nation's
Bar/Bat Mitzvah

At this time, when this sidrah is read in the run-up to the High Holydays, we are urged to take stock of our lives and to make good any of our shortcomings. If, for any reason, our sense of Jewish identity, our religious practice or our synagogue attendance has been weak, now is the time to think deeply about it, and to resolve to improve and to strengthen our religious ties.

For those celebrating a Bar or Bat Mitzvah this is a most appropriate time for some serious soul-searching, a time to come to terms with the fact that, as a Jew, one is not expected to live a life that is independent of, or remote from, the community. This is why Judaism requires ten males over the age of Bar Mitzvah in order to hold a synagogue service. We do not pray as individuals. We pray as part of a community. We pray for the peace and welfare of the entire community, not just our own.

This particular sidrah conveys this message most forcefully in its opening sentences. In a sense it describes the Bar Mitzvah of the entire Israelite nation. At Sinai they were given the Torah, but, ironically, most of it was not relevant to the generation that received it, because they were not destined to enter the Promised Land. So the vast majority of Torah laws were not applicable to them: laws relating to the monarchy, agriculture, tithes, the Temple, the annual ceremony of bringing the first fruits, laws relating to Israelite and foreign slaves, the laws of the seventh and fiftieth years (*Shemittah* and *Yoveil*), the institution of cities of refuge, legislation governing a city that went over to idolatry, laws relating to property rights and inheritance, and so on.

So Moses waited until the last year of his life before addressing the younger generation, destined to enter Israel under his successor Joshua. And he organized a great and awesome ceremony, wherein the entire nation entered into a covenant with God, to accept his Torah and to be loyal to His will: *Attem nitzavim ha-yom kulchem* ... 'You are all standing here this day before The Lord Your God: your leaders, your tribes, your elders, your officers, all the people of Israel, your little ones, your wives, and the stranger within your gates' ... *le'ovr'cha bivrit Hashem Elokecha* ... 'that you may enter into the covenant with the Lord thy God' (Deuteronomy 29: 9–11).

This was, in essence, a national Bar/Bat Mitzvah ceremony. And every subsequent ceremony of that kind, modelled on that great biblical summons to observe the Torah, similarly takes place in the presence of the community, symbolic of the entire nation of Israel. That is because a Bar/Bat Mitzvah is of the utmost importance to our entire nation. Every Jewish youth has the potential to make a great contribution to our national cause. We all have different skills, strengths and creative ideas. We can all help protect the Jewish people, or enrich it culturally, educationally, artistically or spiritually. We all have a contribution to make, to the land and the people of Israel, and to our local Diaspora communities.

We do not live in our own ivory tower. We live among Jewish communities; and each and every one of us has a role to play, a mission to achieve, a contribution to make, a burden to shoulder and a blessing to dispense.

CHAPTER FIFTY-SEVEN

Vayeilech:
The Jewish model of leadership

Vayeilekh Mosheh, vayedabeir et hadvarim ha-eileh el kol yisrael
– 'And Moses went and spoke all these words to all Israel'

Our commentators ask why the Torah saw fit to draw attention to the fact that Moses 'went' to Israel to teach them the Torah. Rather we would have expected the people to have shown honour to their teacher, Moses, and to have gone to him to receive instruction. Why did they hold back and wait for Moses to seek them out?

One answer is that it was not a lack of respect on the part of the people. Quite the contrary: it was a mark of their great love for him. They knew that the Torah was to consist of 613 mitzvot. By their calculation, they had already received 611 of these, corresponding to the *gematria* (numerical value) of the word *Torah*. They realized, therefore, that there were but two more mitzvot to be given before Moses had completed his life's mission. The remaining two were the mitzvah of *Hakhel* (Deuteronomy 31: 10–13) – convening a special assembly of the entire nation every seven years for a public reading of the Torah and a ceremony of confirmation of their commitments to it – and the mitzvah of *Kitvu lachem et ha-shirah ha-zo't* (Deuteronomy 31: 19) – making written copies of the Torah so that the entire nation might study it among themselves.

The Israelites, it is suggested, took a conscious decision not to assemble before Moses in order to delay the moment when he would have to teach them the final two mitzvot. They knew that once that had been done, Moses would have to depart this world. In their overwhelming desire to keep their beloved leader with them as long as possible, they waited for Moses to come to them, rather than go to him for instruction in those two mitzvot.

Moses knew that the Israelites could not enter the Promised Land until they had received all 613 mitzvot. When their ploy to delay receiving the last two mitzvot dawned on him, Moses *hastened* (*Vayeilech*) to the Israelites in order not to hold back for a moment their entry into the land of Israel. Moses was totally unconcerned at the fact that he was hastening his own death thereby.

So we have in this sidrah a classical example of the great love that Israel had for their leader and teacher on the one hand, and the total love and utterly selfless devotion – to the extent of sacrificing life itself – that Moses displayed toward them. Whether we are leaders or followers we can learn much from that mutual love.

When we reflect on secular leadership and the behaviour of politicians in our age we are confronted, in most countries, with double standards, corruption, backbiting rivalry, self-promotion and downright misrepresentation of fact. When we review the life of our great national leader, Moses, on the other hand, we meet a great paragon of virtue, consideration, self-sacrifice, humility and righteousness. That is the Jewish model of leadership. Those are the values to which we are all challenged to aspire.

CHAPTER FIFTY-EIGHT

Ha'azinu:
Not every situation is reversible

Young adulthood means being at a level of maturity when one can appreciate that life is 'not just a bowl of cherries', exclusively carefree, and that there are many people who inevitably have to face some very stressful, even tragic, situations, such as divorce, ill health or disability in the family, loss of livelihood, domestic stress and violence, or death of a loved one. Even young people are not immune, and often may bear the consequences of their parents' or siblings' suffering in those situations. There are also a host of problems that are part and parcel of growing up, such as the perception that parents do not 'understand' them, such as the effects of bullying at school, such as feeling excluded from their friends' circle, teachers who seem to 'take it out on them', problems of 'relationships', important exams that they fear they might fail. The list is endless.

This opens up the question of how to deal with life's setbacks. A child simply cries when he or she is unhappy. Adults also occasionally cry, but, unlike the child, they know that their tears will only grant them a temporary emotional release, but will not solve problems! The adult knows that he or she has to adopt a more realistic and constructive way of dealing with problems once the tears have dried up. If the issue is financial, they know that they have to look afresh at their situation, perhaps by cutting down on unnecessary expenses, taking fewer holidays, maybe even downsizing on their home and car. If the problem is legal they will consult a good lawyer; if it is medical or emotional they will seek the best professional help available; if personal, they may discuss it with a trusted and wise friend or sit back and rethink their own role in the relationship that may have deteriorated. If the problem is spiritual they may consult their rabbi.

It is also important to realize that some problems have no 'solution', but simply involve self-adjustment and accommodating to a new reality, a changed set of circumstances, a slightly less happy or cosy environment, or a need for greater self-reliance rather than leaning on a partner, spouse, friend or associate.

Not every situation is reversible, and in the sidrah Ha'azinu Moses demonstrates precisely how to face up to adversity. He had to 'accept' the divine sentence that, because he struck the rock instead of speaking to it, he would never enter the Promised Land (see Numbers 20: 12). But the way he accepted it discloses the unique quality of his faith and the depth of his maturity and courage. Any lesser national and spiritual leader would certainly have been depressed as the end of his life approached, and he contemplated the failure of his greatest dream and life's mission – to see his people settled in the land to which he had been leading them for forty years. Any lesser leader would have found it almost impossible to prevent his inevitable feeling of resentfulness from infiltrating his final leave-taking speech to his people.

But what approach did Moses take? First, to publicly affirm God's absolute justice in all His decisions: *Hatzur tamim pa'olo* – 'As for the mighty (divine) Rock, His deeds are perfect, for all His ways are totally just. He is a God of faithfulness, without fault; He is just and fair' (Deuteronomy 32: 4). It is clear that Moses was attempting to silence the many Israelite voices who must have found it incomprehensible that God could not forgive a man as loyal and holy as Moses, and would deprive him of his most cherished wish.

Not every situation is reversible. Moses was mature enough to know and to accept that. Maybe God had explained to him, when Moses was with Him on Sinai, exactly why He had to stand by His original decision. Maybe He did not. Either way, Moses did not entertain even a shadow of doubt that 'He is a God of faithfulness, without fault ... just and fair'. That Moses was not just 'paying lip-service' to that notion, but passionately believed that God's decision to take him to heaven prematurely was absolutely just, and would bring perfect bliss to his immortal soul, is clear from his happy state of mind as he took his leave of Israel. This is reflected in his leave-taking speech to his people which constitutes the sidrot of *Ha'azinu* and *V'zot ha-brachah*. This was not couched in formal and serious prose, reflecting a sombre, distracted or doubting mood, but rather in the form of joyous, poetic songs of praise.

Moses had clearly worked very hard on the preparation of that final address. Its style is flowing and expansive, its vocabulary rich and colourful; the metre of every line measured and contrived. Dramatic and penetrating are its allusions to the grandeur of nature, the contemplation of the Creation, Israel's earlier history, God's close protection of His people, as well as the lengthy denunciation of Israel's ingratitude in the face of all that God had done and provided for them. This was the speech of a man still totally focused on his mission and his calling, still, as ever, God-intoxicated, and in no way distracted by his personal situation or self-centred ambitions.

Moses could never have set himself the task of teaching Israel the meaning of gratitude at such a time had he, himself, harboured even a tinge of ingratitude:

> How could you deal with the Lord in such a manner,
> You foolish and thoughtless people?
> Is not He the father that brought you into existence?
> Did He not nurture you and establish you? (Deuteronomy 32: 6).

What an important message this sidrah contains for those about to embark on the exciting yet turbulent voyage of discovery through adult life. There is a Chinese proverb that, 'one cannot prevent the birds of sorrow flying around one's head, but one *can* prevent them nesting in one's hair'. Moses taught us how to deal with setbacks, adversity and the dashing of our most cherished hopes. Throughout his ministry he had to contend with people's jealousy, anger, rejection, insults, even violence, as well as having been burdened with his own self-doubts. The one thing he never doubted, however, was the absolute justice of God. He demonstrated that coping with life is all about developing a mature attitude, viewing life as it is, not necessarily as we would like it to be. A child is entitled to want to live in a make-believe world. An adult is not.

CHAPTER FIFTY-NINE

V'zot Ha-brachah:
Being a fully-rounded Jew

Unlike all the other complete sidrot of the Torah, which are read exclusively on Sabbaths, this final sidrah has a special festival day reserved for its reading, namely *Simchat Torah*, the Rejoicing of the Law. This 'rejoicing' derives from the sense of achievement involved in the completion of an annual cycle of reading and learning, and it, in turn, inspires the *siyyum*, 'celebration of *completion*', when an individual or a study circle has completed the learning of an entire section of the Mishnah or a volume of the Talmud.

There has been a remarkable revival in Jewish learning over the past fifty years, with countless yeshivot and girls' seminaries having been established all over the world, especially in Israel. These cater for all standards, and attract students after they have completed their secondary school education. Such a blend of secular education and Torah study makes for a fully-rounded Jew, able to bring a deeper and broader perspective into the study of both.

A great nineteenth-century rabbi, commentator and philosopher, Samson Raphael Hirsch, promoted this synthesis of Torah and secular culture – *Torah im derech eretz* – as the ideal to which we should aspire. To ensure that this did not remain a mere concept, but that generations of Jews in Germany would be reared in that religious approach, he established a school in 1853. Although a Chief Rabbi, and burdened with all the demands of his office, he personally acted also as director of his school for the first five years of its existence. His school was opposed by the Reform

169

community as well as by most of his Orthodox followers, who refused to send their children there. Hirsch himself had to go from house to house, raising funds and persuading his community to support his institution and its philosophy.

He expressed that philosophy most clearly in an open letter to his Reform opponents, written in 1854:

> Since Judaism encompasses the whole of man, and, in keeping with its explicit mission, promotes the happiness of the whole of mankind, it is wrong to confine its teachings to the Bet ha-Midrash (house of study) or within the home of the Jew. Our Jewish identity demands that our perspectives and objectives become universal. We must not be a stranger to anything that is good, true and beautiful in art and in science, in civilisation and in learning. We must receive with joy and blessing everything of truth, justice, peace and the ennobling of man, wherever it be revealed ... We must dedicate ourselves with joy to every true advance in civilisation and enlightenment, on the condition that this never obliges us to sacrifice our Judaism, but rather to fulfil it with even greater perfection. (Leo Jung, *Guardians of Our Heritage*, New York, 1958, p. 290)

Over two centuries after Hirsch had his dream of ridding European Jewry of its narrowness of mind and of its belief that the Jew had to totally separate himself from secular culture in order to survive, there is a growing and powerful trend today to 'put the genie back in the bottle', and return to that narrow, medieval attitude of mind. Orthodox Judaism today is greatly divided, with the philosophy of *charediut*, extremism and separatism, becoming more and more dominant, and with a growing number of sects and groups refusing to allow their children to have a good secular education or attend university. Those of us who are members of mainstream Orthodox communities must not be pressurized into thinking that we have to adopt a certain uniformity of dress, image and lifestyle or that we must withdraw from participation in the civic life of our general community. If there is discrimination against women in our religious circle, if there is a less-than-positive attitude to Israel, a denigration of non-Jews or a smug sense of religious superiority in our community, then it is our responsibility to protest in the strongest of terms. Such attitudes run counter to the letter and the native spirit of our faith.

Our beloved state of Israel is the ultimate expression of Jewish identity. It is our pride and the agency of security for every Jew throughout the world. Yet there are those, such as the Neturei Karta Chasidic sect in Jerusalem and the vast Satmar sect in Williamsburg, who claim to represent the purest expression of Orthodox values, but who vehemently oppose the State of Israel. Some of their members have actively aligned themselves, and join demonstrations with, the terrorist organizations that seek to destroy the land and the people of Israel! Their attitude to their less religious brethren, as well as to the world of non-Jews, is totally negative, some might say racist. They divorce themselves from the world, and do not give a thought as to its problems and its destiny.

Such an attitude is a travesty of Jewish values. Let us not forget that when God brought our people out of Egypt, He also allowed the 'mixed multitude', of foreigners who had been wrongly imprisoned by the Egyptians, to make good their escape together with Israel (Exodus 12: 38), even though He knew that this particular group would prove to be a bad influence. How much less, then, dare we do anything to endanger the confidence and security of our own brethren!

So, as we conclude another annual Torah cycle, let us consider well the challenge of leading a Torah life, what it demands of us, and what many today falsely allege are its demands. It most definitely provides a blueprint for us to be fully-rounded Jews: to interact with the world, to care for it and for our own particular society, and to play our part in contributing toward its progress, peace, security and values. It calls on us to immerse ourselves in our Torah, to live by its moral and ethical principles and to be a 'light to the nations' around us. The promised result of that way of life will be that, 'the peoples of the world will see that the name of God is reflected in you, and they shall have respect for you' (Deuteronomy 28: 10).

This is the challenge the Torah presents to all young Jews: to become 'fully rounded', by internalizing the philosophy of *Torah im Derech Eretz*, a Torah way of life suffused with cultured, modern living and the highest possible level of achievement and integrity in one's professional or business life. It is also a call to reach out to all God's children and, through our skills and our moral conviction, to help improve their lot and to bring credit to the Jewish name. It is certainly a call to live in the world, to help repair it, and not to recoil from it.

That this calls for courage and determination is without doubt. Our contribution will certainly be resented in many quarters, our purpose will be misconstrued and our achievements denied. But that must never deter us. That this calls for great reserves of inner strength adds resonance to the words with which we conclude this final sidrah (and the conclusions of the four previous books of the Torah): *Chazak chazak v'nitchazeik*, 'Be strong, be strong, and let us harness the God-given strength innate within each and every one of us.'

PART SIX

SPECIAL OCCASIONS, FESTIVALS,
ANNIVERSARIES AND INTERESTS

CHAPTER SIXTY

Bar/Bat Mitzvah –
not Bar/Bat Torah or
Bar/Bat Mitzvot

O ur rabbis had a choice of titles available to them when they first bestowed the title Bar Mitzvah, literally, 'son of the commandments', upon 13-year-olds being called to the Torah for the first time. Significantly, they did not use the more obvious and appropriate title, Bar Torah ('son of the Torah'), which, interestingly, was a popular term in Aramaic (*bar uryan*) to describe a scholar. They appreciated that to give such a grand title to a young boy would imply a commitment to, and mastery of, the entirety of the Torah, which was clearly inappropriate in one so young. They also refrained from applying the much more accurate term, Barmitzvot (plural), 'son of the commandments', perhaps because that indicated an obligation to observe all the mitzvot of the Torah. This may have been fine as an ideal, but the rabbis knew that it was unattainable.

They were far from naive. As teachers, they knew the shortcomings as well as the strengths of the younger generation, so they did not set targets that they knew were impossible to achieve, and hence they refused to bestow premature praise or honorific religious titles. They were even harsh on themselves. The ultimate accolade that a distinguished sage can achieve is to be called *talmid chacham*, which can be translated as either 'a wise student', or merely 'a student of the wise', which shifts the praise on to his teacher, and says nothing of the student's ability.

In the light of this we can understand why they created the title Bar Mitzvah, using the singular noun, meaning, literally, 'son of *a* mitzvah'. This suggests, simply, one who is now subject to the fulfilment of God's law. Exactly how many of those laws he fulfils is his personal challenge. There is no publicly displayed score-sheet and no grandiose title that may ultimately prove an embarrassment if its bearer fails to live up to expectations.

The message is that whatever individual mitzvah the young person may choose to claim as his own, to practise with an extra degree of devotion and loyalty, that of itself is a worthy religious exercise. With one single mitzvah our rabbis believed a person could gain his or her place in heaven.

Indeed, this may be illustrated by a most poignant story in the Talmud (Avodah Zarah 17b) regarding the martyrdom of a great Torah sage, R. Hanina ben Teradyon. The Roman governor had placed damp tufts of wool around his body to prolong his consciousness and pain while he was being burnt at the stake. The executioner, awed by the rabbi's courage and faith, offered to remove the damp material and increase the fire so that death would come much quicker, provided that R. Hanina would guarantee him a place in the World to Come.

The sage agreed. Shortly after the wool was removed and the temperature of the fire increased, Hanina expired, whereupon the executioner himself leaped into the flames. A heavenly voice was heard to proclaim, 'Both Hanina and his executioner have gained an honoured place in the World to Come'. When this was reported to R. Judah the Prince, he exclaimed, 'Some attain their (heavenly) place in an hour, while others only after many years'. Thus the Roman soldier was, in essence, a bar mitzvah, in the sense that he fulfilled but 'one mitzvah', and yet it earned him eternity.

The singular title, Bar mitzvah, 'son of a mitzvah', is thus a gentle call not to be overawed by the vast number of mitzvot – laws, customs, rituals, practices, prayers, blessings and study obligations – that Judaism involves, but to take one mitzvah at a time, to study and research it, and to attempt to fulfil it to the best of one's ability. It may be Kashrut – a ritual whose vast literature forms the main subject on which rabbis are examined for their diploma – or Shabbat, with its complex principles and demanding laws. It may be prayer – to take more time over it and recite it with extra concentration –

or tefillin, not to miss a single day. Or it may be daily Torah study. The message inherent in the name Bar Mitzvah ('son of a mitzvah') is that even if one is only able to become truly informed about *one single mitzvah*, that is also a worthy attainment. The obvious hope is that this will become the springboard for the study and practice of many more mitzvot in the years ahead.

This message is equally applicable to young women, to whom we also allocate the title Bat Mitzvah, 'daughter of a mitzvah', rather than employing the plural form Bat Mitzvot. As in the case of boys, the title Bat Torah was not accorded to them, since it implied a mastery of the tradition that, in most cases, could not really be anticipated.

CHAPTER SIXTY-ONE

Baruch shep'tarani:
A father's blessing

There is a none-too-flattering formula prescribed to be recited publicly by the father of a Bar Mitzvah immediately after his son has been called up to the Torah. It reads, *Baruch shep'tarani mei'onsho shel zeh*, which the *Singer's Prayer Book* translates, 'Blessed is He who has freed me from the responsibility for this child'.

Now, while that translation sounds quite inoffensive, it is clearly a paraphrase undertaken to avoid two problems in the Hebrew original. First, there is no word for 'child' in the Hebrew formula, and secondly, the translation of *onsho* by 'responsibility' is also inaccurate, since the word *onesh* actually means 'punishment!'

So, translated literally, *Baruch shep'tarani mei'onsho shel zeh* actually means, 'Blessed be He who has freed me from the punishment of this'.

Now what sort of a way is it to refer to one's son as a *zeh*, a 'this'? *Singers* translation may have toned down the problem by adding the words '(from the responsibility) for this child!' but, as we have observed, the Hebrew original makes no mention of 'child'. So how do we explain that rather derogatory reference to the Bar Mitzvah boy as a *zeh*, a 'this'?

My answer is that the whole sense of this formula lies precisely in its use of the demonstrative pronoun *zeh*, 'this', in a derogatory sense. This will become clearer when we have demonstrated how it is found in that sense in a number of biblical passages.

In the sidrah *Toldot*, we have two such examples. The first occurs when Rebecca, totally depressed and frightened by the mighty struggling and thrashing around that she experiences within her womb as her twin foetuses wrestled with each other, exclaims, *im kein, lamah zeh anochi* (Genesis 25: 22). This is a difficult phrase to translate. The Hertz Chumash renders it freely as, 'if so, why do I live?' I would prefer to render the phrase, *im kein*, 'If it is so' – if they truly are at war with each other – then, *lamah zeh anochi*, What sort of a *zeh* – a worthless person – am I (to have deserved such offspring)?'

The second example of *zeh* in this derogatory sense, occurs when Esau returns exhausted from the field, and asks Jacob to give him the mess of pottage. Esau gladly exchanges his birthright for the food, saying to Jacob, 'I am about to die – *v'lamah zeh liy bechorah* – why then do I need this birthright' (25: 32) – this worthless privilege!

A third example occurs in the sidrah *Va-yeitzei*, when Jacob tries to defend his action in fleeing away from his father-in-law Laban's home, with his wives and his children. He lists for Laban all the hardships he had endured during the twenty years he served in his household, and which he could no longer endure. He tells Laban, *Zeh esrim shanah anochi immach*, 'This (stressful) twenty years I have been with you' (Genesis 31: 38), then repeats the sentiment, *Zeh liy esrim shanah b'veitecha* – literally, 'this (trauma) is what I suffered (*zeh liy*) in your house for twenty years' (31: 41). So again, we encounter *zeh* in the derogatory sense.

A fourth example is when the people panicked as Moses, who had been away on Mount Sinai to receive the Torah for forty days and nights, did not return at the expected time. Their anger at Moses was at boiling point, to the extent that they were prepared to make a Golden Calf – as much an attempt to punish Moses as to reject God. They cried out to Aaron, 'Make us a God – *kiy zeh Mosheh ha'ish, lo yada'nu meh hayah lanu* ... because this fellow Moses, we do not know what has become of him' (Exodus 32: 1). We can almost hear all their fear and frustration being poured into that phrase *zeh Mosheh ha'ish*, 'this fellow Moses', 'This no-good!'

It is very significant that Moses picks up on that *zeh* insult, and, a little later, he utilizes the opportunity to hurl it back in the direction from which it came. When God threatens to destroy the people,

Moses pleads for mercy for his people, though he does not minimize the terrible thing they had done. He says *Anna chata ha'am ha-zeh chata'ah gedolah*, 'Indeed, this *worthless* people has sinned grievously' (32: 31).

A sixth, and most telling example of that derogatory sense of *zeh* occurs when the parents of a delinquent bring their child before the courts. There they declaim the formula, *Bneinu zeh sorer umoreh* – 'Our son, this *worthless* fellow, is stubborn and rebellious.'

The last example we shall offer (though there are many more) is from the book of Esther. When Esther discloses to the king the cause of her fear and unhappiness in the face of the enemy attempting to destroy her and her people, King Ahashverosh rises up in fury and demands to know – '*miy hu zeh* – who is that *scoundrel? – v'eizehu* – and what sort of *rogue* is he – *asher m'lao libbo la'a-sot ken* – whose heart would prompt him to perpetrate such an act?' (Esther 7: 5)

We may now return to our original problem, namely the strange formula uttered by the father of the Bar Mitzvah, *Baruch shep'tarani mei-onsho shel* **zeh**. Let us remind ourselves at this point of our second observation that *Singers* has also toned down the meaning of the word, *onsho*, which means 'punishment' or 'suffering', rather than 'responsibility'. With all this in mind we can now understand exactly what the father is saying, and why he refers to his son as a *zeh*.

The formula may now be seen as a thanksgiving by the proud and grateful father, having witnessed his son kissing the Torah, blessing and reading from it, and signifying thereby his acceptance of all the mitzvot and his enthusiastic entry into the ranks of the adult Jewish community. The father expresses these emotions through the recitation of a public thanksgiving: '*Barukh shep'tarani* – Blessed be God who has relieved me – *mei'onsho*, of the punishment – *shel zeh*, of a child that is a *zeh*, a worthless and contemptible character.'

My child, he implies, is the very opposite of a *zeh*. He is a fine, loyal, proud, learned and deeply committed young man, of whom his parents and family may be justly proud.

CHAPTER SIXTY-TWO

She'asani kirtzono:
The challenge of the
Women's Blessing

We are all aware of the variation in the daily morning thanks-giving blessings offered by men and women. Men bless God, *shelo asani isha*, 'for not having made me a woman', with all the extra responsibilities of bearing children and running the home, leaving women much less time for prayer and spiritual pursuits. Women, on the other hand, bless God, *She'asani kirtzono*, 'for having made me according to His will'. There have been a number of attempts to explain the precise meaning of that phrase, for surely men are also made 'according to God's will'.

Some explain that the noun *ratzon*, at the root of the word *kirtzono*, means not only 'will', but also 'favour', as in the popular plea *Yehiy ratzon milfanecha*, 'May it be *favourable* before Thee.' In other words, God gave woman an extra measure of special grace and favour, granting her the privilege of being the fairer sex.

We can also explain *ratzon*, from the verb *ratzah*, in its sense of 'to please', as in the phrase, *Ratzah Ha-Kadosh Baruch Hu lezakot et Yisrael* – 'The Holy One, blessed be He, *was pleased* to confer merit on Israel' (conclusion of each chapter of Ethics of the Fathers).

Baruch ... she'asani kirtzono would then mean, 'God who made me *in the way that was especially pleasing* to Him'. This would be a reference to the fact that Eve was made out of Adam's rib, enabling man and woman, husband and wife, to reach a special relationship within marriage that brings spirituality into their lives in a way that being separate from each other never could. This aspect of the man-woman partnership, that was created when woman came along, obviously 'pleased' God greatly, just as, in the sidra *Bereishit*, we are told that every aspect of each day's creation pleased God, who 'saw that it was good'. Hence, women offer up that thanksgiving blessing which implies that man was only complete when woman came along, and that the creation of woman was, therefore, especially pleasing to God.

But the word *kirtzono*, 'after his will', may also refer back to the first man, and that blessing may mean therefore that God made woman according to *Adam's* will. In Genesis 2: 19–22 we are told that God brought all living species to Adam for companionship, but he found none that was compatible. It was then that God made Eve in a form that was *kirtzono*, perfectly in tune with man's will and desire.

A simpler explanation of *She'asani kirtzono*, which also offers a great challenge to a young woman, is '(Blessed be ...) who made me *to act according to* His will', that is, to do as much as humanly possibly to base my life on what I know God would desire; to prepare myself thoroughly for the noble task of eventually establishing a home based upon religious values, and encouraging my family to observe the mitzvot with joy, pride and enthusiasm.

CHAPTER SIXTY-THREE

For tennis-loving youth

Anyone who knows anything about tennis is aware of the system of 'seeding' which was introduced in the USA as early as 1911. The idea of seeding is that outstanding players, expected to reach the last few stages of the competition, on the basis of their current form and the matches and competitions they have won, are designated as 'seeds', and are placed in certain positions in the draw to ensure that they are not drawn against each other in the early stages of the competition, where they might well knock each other out. Such a situation would mean that inferior players, through the good fortune of being drawn exclusively against players of similar standard, could easily find themselves undeservedly winning through to the final stages, thus depriving the competition of its excitement and fairness. Hence, because the seeds play against the lower-ranking players in the early rounds, we were treated one year to the amazing spectacle of an almost unknown Ivo Karlovic, seeded 203, playing against and defeating the defending champion, Leyton Hewitt in the first round of the 2003 Wimbledon Championship.

Now, if any of my readers are wondering how this relates to a Torah message, I would ask them to consider the famous episode of Korach's rebellion against the leadership of Moses (Numbers ch. 16). In the leadership stakes, Korach was certainly a seeded player. After all, he had championship pedigree. He was the grandson of Aaron; and there was no better or more demanding coach than that. He was surely destined for leadership and greatness. He and his family had the privilege, as Levites, of being in charge of the Sanctuary. Whenever Israel moved camp, it was the task of Levites to dismantle and erect it again at the new station.

Korach enjoyed fame and fortune, as many of the ordinary Israelites would have brought all their thanksgiving offerings and the tithes of their flocks to him. As one of the top seeds he would certainly have been a favourite to win the competition for leadership. He might well have been the favoured candidate to succeed Moses, instead of Joshua.

So what went wrong? Well, it seems that he just wanted to win the championship, the fame and the prize money without putting in the required serious practice. He was not prepared to struggle in the cause of his people and his religion, gain recognition and work his way to the top the hard way. He just wanted the title, without earning it. He was the prototype of the seed who shows great promise, who is expected to do great things, but who does not train with sufficient dedication, does not fulfil his or her potential, turns in a poor performance and gets knocked out in the early rounds.

There is a temptation in some circles to seed Bar and Bat Mitzvahs, and to take it for granted that some will remain, religiously, top seeds throughout their lives, and that others, who, because they have not yet displayed the signs of a deep commitment, will not be seeded. In mainstream Orthodox synagogues we have families representing every level of religious observance. Of course, we make no distinction between them. They are all equally valued, for a variety of reasons, including the important one that religious observance for so many is not a static matter, but is rather like an escalator. Some young men and women – and some not so young – are slowly but surely moving upwards, towards the higher seeded positions, dramatically increasing their commitment to the Torah and observance, while others, who may have been brought up with high standards, are sadly moving downwards, gradually becoming a little more lax in their observances, and, consequently dropping in their seeded positions.

Hence, it is a hazardous exercise to seed Bar or Bat Mitzvahs. Some top seeds, like Hewitt, get knocked out in the first round of the competition. Some Barmitzvah boys, for whom we had great hopes, pack up their tallit and tefillin bags no sooner the Bar Mitzvah day is over, and we do not see them again. Others – especially those encouraged by their parents – just seem to go from strength to strength, achieving greater and greater heights, discovering deeper fulfilment and richness in their lives. A few actually go on to reach the position of top seed, and become rabbinic, educational or lay leaders of our community.

So every year, when Wimbledon arrives, it will be a worthwhile exercise to ask oneself what one imagines one's current religious seed ranking to be, whether one has deepened or loosened one's religious ties, whether one has lived for oneself alone or also for others, and whether one has made a contribution towards the welfare of one's people and the support of our beloved homeland of Israel.

CHAPTER SIXTY-FOUR

For football-loving youth

Quite a few of our sidrah messages have referred to that most important challenge for young people: making the most of their potential. As messages may be derived from a wide variety of life's situations and contexts, perhaps now that we have utilized all the sidrot we may exploit humour as a source of inspiration.

It is related that, at the height of the Intifada, the Israelis and Arabs realized that, if they continued, they would some day end up destroying the world. So they sat down and decided to settle the whole dispute with a dog fight.

The negotiators agreed that each country would be given five years to develop the best fighting dog possible, and that the one that won the fight would earn its country the right to occupy Israel, with the losing side having to lay down its arms.

The Arabs found the biggest, meanest Dobermans and Rottweilers in the world. They bred them together and then crossed their offspring with the meanest Siberian wolves. They used steroids and trainers in their quest for the perfect killing machine, until, after the five years were up, they had a dog that needed iron prison bars on his cage. Only the trainers could handle this beast.

When the day of the big fight arrived, the Israelis showed up with a strange animal: it was a nine-foot-long Dachshund. Everyone felt sorry for the Israelis. No one thought for a moment that this weird and unwieldy animal stood a chance against the growling beast in the Arab camp, and the bookies predicted the Arabs would win in less than a minute.

The cages were opened. The Dachshund waddled toward the centre of the ring. The Arab dog leapt from his cage and charged. As he got to within an inch of the Israeli dog, the Dachshund opened its jaws and swallowed the Arab beast in one bite. There was nothing left but a small bit of fur from the killer dog's tail.

The Arabs approached the Israelis, shaking their heads in disbelief. 'We do not understand. Our top scientists and breeders worked for five years with the meanest, biggest Dobermans and Rottweilers. They developed a veritable killing machine.'

'Really?' the Israelis replied. 'We had our top plastic surgeons working for five years to make an alligator look like a Dachshund!'

The moral of the story is that things are not necessarily as they appear in life. It is that we should never be surprised by the power and ingenuity of the creative imagination and of the potential that lies within man which, if properly harnessed, can enable him to achieve the impossible. But we also have to believe in ourselves, and we have to recognize our strengths and constantly work on them. For if we press hard on the gates of our individual potential, they will open wider than we ever imagined.

So many young people today are wasting the potential within them, not realising that it is a fierce and competitive world out there where everyone has to give of their very best if they wish to succeed. If half the time, energy, passion and money that the nation poured into football was invested into self-development and community service, we would have a model society.

Instead, we have a world that defines itself largely in relation to football. Men who have special skills in kicking around a ball are the real heroes of society. Not the world's political or religious leaders, not the Nobel prize-winners who truly take society forward in so many important fields – the men of literature who inspire our thoughts and emotions, and the men of science and medicine who directly improve the quality of our lives. No, not them. Their names are almost totally unknown to the world. But ask them to list the stars of the English, Italian and German national football teams, and even their managers and coaches, and they will spring into animated and informed discussion.

Can that obsession be healthy? Can a hooligan of a footballer, who head-butts an opponent in a world cup final, be a suitable role model for young people?

So what is the message? It is that of the dachshund and the alligator. The Arabs in that joke saw only a dachshund, and they thought they were on to a winner. They didn't realise that that was just the outer shell. Indeed, our *Pirkei Avot*, Ethics of the Fathers, advises us, *Al tistakeil bekankan ela b'mah sheyesh boh*, 'Do not look at the outer vessel, but at what is inside' (4: 27). We should never be fooled by, or make judgements on the basis of, outward appearances. Neither should we become obsessed by shallow role models who may have the capacity to entertain and excite, but never to really enrich, inspire or improve our own human skills and character development.

CHAPTER SIXTY-FIVE

For cricket-loving youth

Many of our young people, including, increasingly, girls, enjoy a game of cricket. Some positively excel at playing, while a larger proportion may not play much but do have considerable interest in the game, especially in the international test matches. I have to admit to a lifetime's interest in watching the game. Jews' College, one of the institutions where I studied to become a rabbi, was within walking distance of the home of cricket, Lord's Cricket Ground, which might well have been one of the reasons why I opted to study at that particular college!

Cricket is a most complex and absorbing game. Unlike a football match that is compressed into ninety minutes, cricket can be drawn out for as long as five days. The swings of fortune during that period can be dramatic, with either side appearing to have the advantage at any given stage, only to have it snatched from them due to an inspired bowling spell or a dogged batting partnership that cannot be dislodged. It is a game where the quality of the pitch, the light or even the weather can give advantage to either the batsman or the bowler, and where field setting is of crucial importance and has to be determined according to the type of delivery (spin or pace) and the trap being set in order to exploit a batsman's weakness at any given time.

Cricket probably has more *dinim* (rules and regulations) than any other sport. There is also an annual called *Wisden Cricketers' Almanack*, that publishes full statistics of the performance of every player in the regular county games, the one-day internationals and the test matches. As with football, people have wildly differing, and vehemently voiced, views on the relative greatness of players and whether the selectors were wise to choose or overlook them for particular matches.

Cricket is very much 'a gentleman's game', not a contact sport. However, with a fast bowler hurling a very hard ball at a batsman at over eighty miles an hour, many would regard it as far more dangerous than football. Unlike football, it is a 'fair weather game', which is not played in the rain, a game from which one generally comes away in a most relaxed frame of mind, having enjoyed not only the play, but also the walk around such wonderful grounds as Lord's during the lunch and the tea intervals. The social interaction with fellow lovers of the game is pleasant, and crowd violence and abuse of players and opposition supporters is almost unknown.

There are many lessons that the game offers to young people in general, as well as some points of contact with specifically Jewish values. We shall content ourselves with but a few.

We have referred to the 'bible' of the game, the book of *Wisden*, wherein are recorded for posterity scorecards detailing the performance of every player in every county and test match game, the highest batting, bowling and catching averages for that season, as well as the career-best performances. The record goes back to the period of the legendary W.G. Grace.

Judaism has a similar concept, of records kept by God covering every single act that humans have performed each year: whether they have striven to lead a better life and to clock up a higher score of mitzvot, or whether they have underperformed by comparison with previous years. The *Pirkei Avot* (2: 1) states *v'chol ma'asecha ba-sefer nichtavim*, 'all your deeds are recorded in a book'; and the Talmud actually speaks of all those individual records subsequently being fed into a vast statistical pool, enabling God to compile three separate records, one listing the names of all the righteous on earth, one with the names of all the really wicked, and the third with the names of all those who are categorized as average (Tal. Rosh Ha-shanah 16b).

A batsman (or batswoman!) who, after making contact with the ball, runs between the wickets (twenty-two yards) scores one run. If, however, he hits the ball to the boundary he scores a four, or a six if it reaches there without bouncing. Judaism also has a system of boundaries. Again we may refer to the *Pirkei Avot* which states *Va'asu seyag la-Torah*, 'Make boundaries around the Torah' (1:1). The boundaries are the precautionary measures which the rabbis have put in place around the Torah prohibitions to ensure that they are not inadvertently transgressed. If we all make boundaries in our moral lives, and insist that the game stops once that boundary has been reached, we are less likely to discredit ourselves.

There is a lesson to be learnt from the spin bowler who turns the ball with his wrist and flights it with his fingers or arm position in a way that, although it initially moves in one direction or bounces in one place on the pitch, it suddenly and unexpectedly changes direction during the last few seconds. The batsman has already mentally prepared himself, and the position of his bat, to make one stroke, so he must make an instantaneous change if he is to avoid the ball hitting his stump or giving a catch to a close-in fielder. Often the ball seems to be going wide of the wicket, and the batsman can be totally mystified as to whether, how and where, it will turn, and how high it will bounce.

It is the same with life. Most of us have a shrewd sense of the right direction we should face, and the nature of the things that life throws at us. We know that we will encounter 'spin bowling', and that there are many so-called friends or acquaintances around who will attempt to mislead us, only appearing as if they are bowling a straight ball at us – relating honestly and morally towards us – when they are, in fact, as deceptive as the spin bowler attempting to trap the batsman unawares.

Wickets are made out of wood. Wood is also a symbol of the Torah: 'It is a tree of life to those that hold firm to it' (Proverbs 3: 18). We should all be aiming straight for the Torah, without deviating, like the fast bowler who bowls straight, with perfect line and length, and hits the wicket with his first bowl. This is not always so easy, however. There are inevitably those who stray, and bowl terribly wide, aiming for objectives that are wide of the Torah's mark. However, all is never lost, for, if one bowls a wide ball, although he concedes a run, yet he also has to bowl that ball again. That is a mixed blessing, since it also means that he has another chance of correcting his direction and hitting the stumps with the next ball.

Every player has to put in hours of practice each day in the nets before he goes onto the field of play. Judaism believes that this world is like the practice nets. It is the place where we must learn all the regulations and perfect every aspect of the game of life, in readiness to earn our place in the first team. 'This world is like a corridor into the World to Come. Prepare yourself in the corridor so that you may enter the inner chamber' (Pirkei Avot 4: 21).

Just as there are test matches wherein the greatest teams that countries can field are matched against each other, so God 'tested' Abraham to see how he ranked in comparison to all the other righteous people in the world. Abraham consistently came out top; and that is why he is regarded as the founder of our people, and the one whose character we admire most and whose values we strive to emulate.

We are told not to believe in ourselves until our very last day on earth (Pirkei Avot 2: 5). The analogy of a cricket match demonstrates the truth of that. So often it occurs that a match is won or lost on the final ball. Often the score that is required in the last few remaining hours of a match, and the run-rate that would have to be achieved for the batting side to win, appears unattainable. And yet, a scintillating performance by the pair at the wicket – occasionally even the tail-enders – exceeds all expectation. Conversely, the tried batsmen may seem to have their eye so well in that the score to be reached for victory seems well within their grasp, given the overs remaining. And yet, totally unexpectedly, wickets suddenly start tumbling in quick succession and the situation is reversed.

We must not imagine that our righteousness and our reputations will always be sustained. So often we encounter men and women, who were held in the highest public esteem for decades, having a sudden moral or ethical breakdown, and destroying the sure and proud reputation they had built up. We should not rest on our laurels, or relax our moral grip, until the last ball of life has been bowled!

One final message: in life, as in cricket, the umpire's decision is final. The divine Umpire has given us the rules and regulations, clearly stated in our Torah. If we fall foul of those rules, He will lift His finger, and declare us 'Out!' Let us bat, bowl and field confidently, so that no one will ever have to doubt us, and shout 'howzat?'

CHAPTER SIXTY-SIX

For American baseball-
loving youth

My British readers may or may not be acquainted with American baseball, a game that has been described by a Jewish philosopher, Morris Raphael Cohen, as 'a national religion'. Such a designation justifies my employing this game as a source for a religious message.

The game should not really be strange since, in addition to major games being broadcast on some of our television channels, it is also clearly based on the game we know as rounders. Nine players from each side go in to bat against the 'pitchers', with the away team batting first, and the winner being the team that scores the most 'runs'. From the perspective of the batters, their aim is obviously to try to achieve a 'home run', rather than a mere move to the first or second base, and to strike the ball beyond the reach of any potential outfielder catchers, giving them time and opportunity to clear all four bases of the diamond-shaped pitch.

This may not sound too challenging for a professional batter, capable of reading the direction, spin or swing, and the velocity of the ball being pitched at him, and especially as – unique to baseball – on the spot guidance is also available from the manager and 'first and third base coaches' positioned in close proximity to play. And, indeed, some present-day classic players, such as Mark McGwire, Sammy Sosa and Roger Maris, have finished seasons with totals of around seventy home runs.

But in baseball's early period, at the beginning of the twentieth century, scoring a home run was truly a rare feat. This was not because of the greatness of the pitchers, but because of the prohibitive cost of baseballs. Club owners were loathe to spend the equivalent in today's money of around US$70 for a ball, so that one ball had to last the entirety of a game, by the end of which it would be misshapen and lumpy and dark with grass and mud. With a ball in such a condition, it proved almost impossible to flight it far enough to score a home run. This period is accordingly referred to as 'The dead ball era'.

Speaking of cash-strapped club owners leads us, by association, to refer to the black baseball players for whom the road was truly hard. An article on the history of baseball in the online encyclopedia *Wikipedia* states that, 'Many towns had whites-only hotels and restaurants. Black players slept in the homes of fans on good days, on the bus, in a barn, or the booth of a ... bar on not-so-good ones, and out in open fields on bad ones. Sometimes they had to keep moving rather than stop for a meal where none could be found' (*Wikipedia*, 'History of Baseball in the United States', p. 8).

In addition, they suffered from almost total exclusion from the white league games until as recently as 1947, forcing them to establish their own Negro leagues. Perhaps, in addition to blind bigotry, it was also fear of the superior skills of the black players that contributed to such a discriminatory attitude.

Such discrimination should not surprise Jews in Britain where most golf clubs excluded Jews, either overtly or covertly, leading to the establishment of Jewish golf clubs and competitions. In London one premier league football club, Tottenham Hotspur, is known for the Jewish influence within the club, a feature that is regarded as quite unique.

So what can we learn from all this? Well, one clear message is perseverance. I have no doubt that those black players were driven by the dream that one day they would be recognized for their skills, rather than discriminated against for the colour of their skin. They knew that the road would be long and painful, and that, if they won the right to play 'on an even playing field', it would be their children who would be the beneficiaries, not them.

And this is a fundamental Jewish principle, expressed in *Pirkei Avot*: *Lo alecha ha-melachah ligmor, v'lo attah ben chorin lehibateil mimmenah,*

'It is not (necessarily) for you to complete the task, but neither are you free to desist from it' (2: 21). In other words, if we sense that the challenge is too formidable for us to complete on our own, we must not despair and abandon it as unattainable. We must still play our part, enabling others to build on what we have contributed, and to enjoy the fruit of success.

This is exemplified in a Midrash which relates that the Emperor Hadrian was travelling through Judea when he came across a very old man planting a carob tree, which takes years to produce fruit.

'Silly man', he called out, 'Are you expecting to live long enough to eat of its fruit?'

'No, great emperor', answered the old man, 'but just as my ancestors planted so that I might enjoy the fruits of their labours, so am I planting for my descendants'.

A similar lesson may be derived from the objective of gaining a 'home run'. Of course that is a most impressive strike, but, like most things in life, we should never assume that success is a matter of 'all or nothing'. The batter who scores his 'run' only after progressing gradually base by base has also made a valuable contribution to his team effort. And it is the same in life. Of course there are 'high fliers', brilliant people, who effortlessly strike their home runs, notching up successes and achieving all their objectives. But, more often, it is the student of average intelligence who 'touches every single base' – is diligent and conscientious in his or her studies, course work and revision, or the professional who displays admirable personal qualities and a sense of responsibility and maturity – who will rise higher and faster up the ladder of advancement.

The third message is to be derived from the batter who requires great skill to anticipate the direction, spin, swing or speed of the ball being hurled at him. That hard ball is truly a missile, and woe betide a batter who misjudges it. (Indeed, it was after the tragic death of the batter, Ray Chapman, on 16 August 1920, who could not see the badly discoloured ball and was struck on the temple, that the era of the dead ball was brought to an end and the rule brought in that umpires must change the ball as soon as it becomes scuffed or discoloured.)

This is a message of vigilance, which is of special importance for young people. In today's dangerous world, all people – but especially Jews – must be extremely vigilant, and realize that, like the ball which, leaving the pitcher's hand, appears to be travelling in a straight direction but may actually be a wicked curve ball, so in life, situations and people are not necessarily how they appear. First appearances – and even subsequent ones – can be extremely deceptive, and we have to be sure that our acquaintances are well and truly 'tried' before we bring them into our inner circle of close friends and trust them with our confidences. We also require to exercise vigilance when it comes to our physical security. Since 9/11 we have entered the age of global terrorism, and we cannot be too careful. It pays to keep our eyes open and to make security our number one priority.

The fourth lesson is just how adversity and discrimination – as suffered by both blacks and Jews – has been a spur to greater achievement rather than a handicap. Things that come too easily are not appreciated, and those who have no tension in their life rarely achieve much. It is a truism that most of the very greatest artists and composers lived in abject poverty. Indeed, once again *Pirkei Avot* reminds us that the way to become an illustrious Torah scholar is, *pat ba-melach tokhal umayyim bamsorah tishteh*, 'to eat bread and salt and to take measured amounts of drink' (6: 4). The same may be said of great achievement in any other field.

So when trials and tribulations come – and who in life is immune to them? – we should view them as challenges to be welcomed, as hurdles to be cleared, as life experiences to be turned to our advantage if they open our eyes to the realities of life and, in turn, make us more mature and sensitive to the problems being faced by our fellow men and women.

Also flowing from this issue of adversity and discrimination is the message, to Jews in particular, to try to ensure that we help protect others from those terrible experiences that we have suffered in such abundance throughout our history. As the great teacher Hillel expressed it so pithily, *Mah d'alach sanei lechavrach la tavid*, 'What is hateful to you do not do to your neighbour' (Talmud Shabbat 31a).

We have learnt some profound lessons from synthesizing

Judaism and baseball. Judaism can provide profound teachings for all the issues and experiences of life: *Hafoch bah v'hafoch bah, dikulah bah,* 'Turn the Torah over and turn it over again, for everything is in it!' (*Pirkei Avot* 5: 28)

CHAPTER SIXTY-SEVEN

For a budding actor

As a rabbi I have addressed young people whose great love is acting (and which youngster is not an actor?), and a few who have already appeared in television plays.

There is, truly, an actor in all of us. Subconsciously, we all act out in our everyday lives one or more roles, either that we are comfortable with or which project the image we would like to present to those around us. From infancy, we pattern ourselves on others: parents, teachers, older brothers or sisters. We borrow their words and mannerisms; we dress or wear our hair like them; often we even borrow their views, their likes and dislikes. We 'act out' their part.

As we get into our teens, we are conditioned by an ever-widening environment. We mould ourselves on those we look up to, especially those whom we perceive that others look up to: the school prefects, the local heroes, youth club leaders, sports and media stars. And we 'act out' their part.

When parents want to show their child that they disapprove of some aspect of his or her behaviour, they also 'act out' the role of an angry person. And when the child wants to demonstrate to its parent that it regards what they have said or done as unfair, it may also 'act out' a tantrum, frequently giving a most brilliant performance, worthy of a British Academy of Film and Television Arts (BAFTA) award.

A psychologist at Bristol University, Dr Susan Blackmore, published a work entitled *The Meme Machine* (Oxford University Press,

1999). 'Memes' are what we copy from each other. As children we see those around us tying their shoelaces, eating with a knife and fork, smiling at each other; and the infant becomes an actor, and imitates those things as accurately as possible, honing his or her performance with each succeeding day. According to Dr Blackmore, it is not only genes which make us what we are, but also our capacity to absorb memes. And the fact that humans have larger brains than other species, is, she suggests, because we are 'Meme machines', the best at imitation, so that our brains have had to expand greatly in order to provide an adequate storage and retrieval system for the vast number of memes that we make use of in expressing ourselves and developing our personality.

One of Dr Blackmore's observations is that religion is a particularly rich source of memes, providing us with a host of experiences, rituals, challenges, role models and modes of conduct which we unconsciously absorb and employ in order to locate and choose the best script for our lives and, within it, the part that we feel is best suited to us.

Our society is, unfortunately, not too discriminating in its choice of memes, and a very high proportion of young people prefer to imitate the lifestyle of unworthy 'role models'. They naively imagine that if such 'stars' are paid a fortune for the skills they possess, then their lives must be equally rich, rewarding and exciting.

How can our youth appreciate how artificial, empty and unsatisfying is the life of the majority of 'celebrities'? How can they possibly appreciate how vulnerable most of them are to exploitation by others, with the result that they are frequently surrounded by those they cannot trust? How can they know what it is like to be hounded by the press, not to have a life of one's own, not to be able to grow up naturally, with the freedom that our youth so expect and cherish?

The message to any budding actor or actress is to refine their acting capacity, and to look to the Torah as the source of the richest memes upon which to base their development and life. Let them act out the roles of the righteous men whose lives are chronicled in our tradition, making the part of Abraham, the great seeker after God and the lover of mankind, their own. Let them take on the sense of responsibility that Moses, the great deliverer and leader of our nation, had to assume, and embody the persona of Aaron, the unrivalled lover and pursuer of peace.

Above all, let them be perceptive actors, imitating the people and the values that will truly aid their desire to have a happy and fulfilling life, a life which will make them a credit to their faith, their family and their people.

CHAPTER SIXTY-EIGHT

For a young Kohein:
'All you need is love!'

As a *Kohein* (priest), myself, I was always particularly pleased to address a new adult member of my fraternity on the occasion of his Bar Mitzvah. I knew that the boy's father would be even more pleased as there are few more spiritually satisfying experiences than standing in front of the Ark on a festival next to one's son, and together performing *duchaning*, the priestly blessing of the congregation.

The message for a young *Kohein* is simply to take as his mission in life, the pre-condition for the privilege of administering that blessing. The rabbis point to the formula of the blessing over the *duchaning*: 'Blessed be God who has commanded us – *levareich et ammo Yisrael be'ahavah* – to bless his people Israel with love.' They derive from this final word the rule that any priest who does not harbour loving feelings for his people, or, conversely, an unpopular priest, should not perform the blessing.

During the Temple period, the priest's love for his people was translated into a dedicated 'calling'. He was expected to work selflessly in the cause of his people, to make great sacrifices for them, just as his ancestors had done when they were denied a tribal share of the land of Israel in order to devote all their time to the spiritual and welfare needs of the nation.

Such demands are not expected any more, but the principle lives on in the form of an extra measure of dedication and devotion to synagogue and community life that is expected of a priest. He is called to the Torah first, and he blesses the congregation 'with love'. The Hebrew word for 'love' – *ahavah* – is associated with the word *hav*, meaning 'to give', 'contribute'. In Judaism, love is not a mere emotion. It is a commitment.

The rabbis ask the question, if the priests are blessing the people, who blesses the priests? Their answer is that God Himself promised to do just that. In the verse where He calls upon the priests to bless the people in His name (Numbers 6: 27), He concludes, *va'ani avarcheim*, 'and I will bless them' (the priests). What more could one ask?

If we bless others, God blesses us. What a simple, yet sublime, message.

CHAPTER SIXTY-NINE

'The Three Weeks':
You can always find time

The fast of the seventeenth of Tammuz inaugurates the three weeks of semi-mourning for the siege of Jerusalem and the destruction of our Bet Ha-mikdash, the ancient Temple, symbol of our religious and national independence. The second Temple was destroyed by the Romans in the year 70 CE. Inevitably, our sages asked themselves what terrible sin could possibly have justified such a punishment, and they concluded that it was the sin of sin'at chinam, causeless hatred of fellow Jews.

The great Rav Kuk used to say that if we want that Temple to be rebuilt and our full sovereignty to be restored we first have to establish peace and harmony among ourselves. We have to be united by cords of respect, concern and love for each other, and replace that destructive sin'at chinam, causeless hatred, with ahavat chinam, causeless love. Our hearts have to overflow with charitableness towards and concern for fellow Jews, whether or not they have engendered such feelings through their treatment of us. By our consideration we have to atone for the sin of the generation whose hard-heartedness caused us to forfeit our Temple.

The late Lubavitcher Rebbe related a true story that links up with the theme of the sidrah Balak and the heathen prophet Bilaam's desire to curse our people. A rabbi once publicly and bitterly attacked the Rebbe for something he is alleged to have said and done. When it was demonstrated to the critic that his informant had totally misrepresented what the Rebbe had said or done, he immediately wrote a letter of apology to the great sage, imploring him not to bear a grudge against him for his rash and false outburst.

'I assure you', replied the Rebbe, 'that I simply do not have the time to bear grudges'; and at all times he attempted to persuade his followers to adopt that attitude. 'How does one possibly find the time to bear grudges?', he would ask. 'How does one find the time and energy to hate? Time is holy and precious. It has to be employed constructively: to love, to dispense kindness, to cement friendships, to bring people closer to God. In short, to change the world!'

It is amazing how we find time to do the things that interest or entertain us. Busy professionals, for whom people have to wait weeks for an appointment and pay a fortune for their time, yet find the time to travel to home and away football matches, to spend a day or two at the test match or Wimbledon, to read the wad of daily and Sunday newspapers, to go to the theatre or the cinema, to spend hours in front of the television. We find the time to get into arguments, to write harsh letters and send offensive e-mails, to instruct lawyers, just as, in the sidrah, King Balak found the time to engage a professional sorcerer, Bilaam, to curse Israel, and to accompany him up hill and down dale to find the most convenient vantage point from which to curse Israel. Time seems to be in plentiful supply when it is needed in order to hate and hurt others, but is in such short supply when required by others in order to help and support them.

This is the message from this sidrah: Always find time – make time – for the things in life that really matter. Not just for the things that give you pleasure, but for the things that will bring pleasure, relief and comfort to others, particularly the less fortunate. And if you grow up with that sort of philosophy, you will help redeem a troubled world, and bring great joy to your family, your community and your people.

CHAPTER SEVENTY

A Kristallnacht anniversary: Guilty spectators

Each year we commemorate the anniversary of *Kristallnacht*, that fateful night of 9 November 1938 when the Nazis initiated a pogrom against German Jewry. They embarked upon a murderous spree, going on the rampage and smashing the windows and looting the shops of Jewish businessmen, setting fire to synagogues and Jewish communal buildings, attacking Jewish homes, and beating, injuring and murdering the peace-loving residents.

Tragically, anti-Jewish feeling is very much alive once again throughout Europe, a matter that our young adults simply cannot ignore. Sadly they have to face up to life as it is, and leave behind the cosiness of a make-believe world.

So what do we make of the events of *Kristallnacht*? Perhaps the most astonishing thing is how the ordinary inhabitants of Germany and Austria, just stood by and watched while Hitler's mobs went around setting fire to Jewish homes, community buildings and synagogues. No one – neither neighbours, friends, fellow workers nor professional colleagues – felt any sense of outrage. No one organized any public outcry or demonstration. They just watched, as if witnessing a fascinating public spectacle, a Guy Fawkes' Night firework display. They just stood by and stared, as if what was happening was quite natural and intriguing, with no moral implications. The Jew at that moment became depersonalized in the eyes of the general population. For if one stands back and allows one's neighbour to be brutalized, his property destroyed and his life endangered for the sole reason that he

belongs to a different faith, that is but one step away from justify-
ing absolutely any fate that might be meted out to him. That is, in
fact, collusion in the crime. The fires of Kristallnacht inevitably
became the torches that but a few years on lit the crematoria of
the concentration camps.

In Hebrew, the one word, Vayar, means not only 'to look' and
'to see', but also 'to reflect deeply upon', 'to foresee (the moral
implications of what is happening before one's eyes)'. This
explains an otherwise unnecessary repetition of the verb vayar at
the beginning of the sidrah Vayeira (Genesis, ch. 18). Abraham
was sitting at the entrance of his tent in the heat of the day: 'Vayissa
einav vayar [And he lifted up his eyes and saw (three men standing
by him)]; vayar [And he saw] vayarotz likratam [and he ran to meet
them].'

The Torah was clearly referring to two types of 'seeing'. The
first vayar tells us, simply, that Abraham 'saw' them; they caught his
eye. The second vayar tells us that Abraham reflected deeply on the
responsibility that the presence of three tired wayfarers imposed
upon him. He then considered the scope of the mitzvah of hospitality that now presented itself.

From Abraham we learn how to relate to what is going on
around us. He taught us never to be a mere spectator, watching as
people around suffer danger, poverty, famine and devastation.
When we see something, it must never be a simple vayar, a superficial, unfocused glance. The Jew must always take a second vayar,
a truly considered 'look', weighing up the moral implications of
what he sees before him to determine how he can help to relieve
pain or lighten burdens.

This is where the population of Germany, Poland and Austria
were found so criminally wanting. They took just one glance. And
they concluded that the Jews' plight had nothing to do with them.
It was simply not their concern.

It is vital for our young people to take into their adult life the
lesson of the two vayars, so that they will always look, and look
again, at how they can play their part in lightening the burdens of
the less fortunate and in encouraging others to be more caring,
more sharing, more tolerant and more involved. That is the only

way to ensure that *Kristallnacht* will never happen again, and that the world might become a safer, fairer, more tolerant and peaceful place.

The message of the two *vayars* may also be applied to Jewish learning. In that context it advises us not to take just one superficial look at a text, but to study *b'omek uv'iyyun*, analytically and with depth, so as to get to the heart of Torah teaching and to be in a position to apply it to one's life as an observant Jew.

This double *vayar* is perhaps what the ancient sage of the Mishnah, Ben Bag-Bag, had in mind when he said *Hafach bah v'hafach bah di kulah bah*, 'Turn it [the Torah text] over, and turn it over again, for everything is in it' (*Pirkei Avot* 5: 25). In other words, one has to look, consider, reflect, compare and research if one wishes the Torah to fully reveal its truths and its secrets, its majesty and its glory, its guidance and its inspiration. If we adopt that approach, our lives will truly be enriched beyond measure.

CHAPTER SEVENTY-ONE

The run up to Rosh Hashanah:
A truly 'good year'

The run up to Rosh Hashanah is truly special. Already for a few weeks before the festival, people will have been exchanging wishes for the new year, and there is an important message to be derived from that traditional blessing that we exchange. Most people say something like, 'Have a happy and healthy year ahead'. In Yiddish-speaking communities they used to say 'Have a *gebentchter yahr*', 'a blessed year'. But that is not, in fact, the pre-scribed, official Hebrew formula. It reads, *leshanah tovah tikatev*, 'May you be inscribed for a *good* year'.

But what do we mean by a 'good' year? Many people will define that as a year of pleasure and success, of great holidays, enjoyable parties, of travelling all over to watch their favourite football team. Now all that may make for a 'great' year, but it is not a 'good' year. All that may suggest a year of quantity, of filling one's time with every activity, but it is not necessarily a year of quality. It is not a *shanah tovah*, a 'good' year, a year of 'goodness', a year of doing good to others, a year where the amount of support we give to worthy causes is increased, a year wherein our connection to our community and to Israel is strengthened. 'Having a *good* year' does not suggest a year when we work on our own 'goodness', finely honing our manners, the way we speak to parents and teachers, the way we live our lives as Jews and human beings. That is the real meaning of *shanah tovah* – 'a good year'.

Each year, as Rosh Hashanah comes around, we should rethink the real meaning of this seasonal greeting, *leshanah tovah tikatev*, 'May you be inscribed for a *good* year.' We should then ask ourselves what extra 'goodness' we might yet be able to take on board, what vacuum might still exist in our way of life that awaits some 'goodness' to fill. In that way, every year will truly be a *shanah tovah*, a really 'good year'.

CHAPTER SEVENTY-TWO

Chanukah:
Being totally 'dedicated'

There are countless messages to be derived from this multifaceted festival. The most obvious one is about being passionate about one's Judaism. For Chanukah means 'dedication', and Chanukah is a clarion call to be fully, not half-heartedly, 'dedicated'.

When the Greek ruler, Antiochus, outlawed Jewish practice, he had no interest in destroying our people. He simply wanted every Jew totally to assimilate to the pagan values and idolatrous practices of Hellenism. But, ironically, even the vast numbers of non-practising Jews suddenly found themselves outraged by this attempt to deprive them of the religion of their fathers.

It was a curious situation. Their attitude was that if they themselves want to neglect their faith, that is their prerogative. But woe betide any outsider who attempted to force them to abandon it! So, even though at the outset there was no threat to their lives, the threat to their religion was construed by all Jews as a threat to their freedom of choice and their survival. And this way of thinking prompted a swift and passionate return to religious observance on the part of the masses.

So one message of Chanukah is that, unlike our assimilated brethren in those far-off days, we should not let our Jewish consciousness and loyalty be dictated to by the anti-Semites, by the realization that there are many out there who are plotting to destroy our people, our faith and our land.

The love of our youth for their religion, and their commitment to its observance, should flow exclusively from a deepening of their understanding of it and their relationship to it with every passing year. And that can only come about through the close study of our sacred literature and the adoption of the religious way of life. That, in turn, will create a growing enlightenment that, just like the lights of the Chanukah candles, will intensify with each succeeding night.

CHAPTER SEVENTY-THREE

Chanukah:
The Maccabean struggle lives on

The word *Chanukah* means 'consecration' or 'dedication', and is applied to ceremonies to mark the acquisition of a new spiritual status or rank. Hence the term *chanukat hamizbei'ach*, for the ritual of dedicating the newly constructed altar in the Sanctuary (Numbers 7: 11), and *chanukat ha-bayit*, the dedication and blessing of a new Jewish home. So Chanukah is the ideal time for a Bar or Bat Mitzvah and the acquisition of a new religious status. Indeed, the relationship between the two celebrations goes much deeper, since, at one level, a Bar or Bat Mitzvah symbolizes one of the main objectives of the Maccabean struggle, namely religious rededication.

Most of the emphasis that we place on this festival relates to the victory of the priestly Maccabees over the ungodly Greeks. Few realize, however, that there was an earlier, and in many ways more critical, battle that preceded that armed conflict against the Greek-Syrians. That was an internal battle for the hearts and minds of young Jewish boys and girls. From the historical account in the Book of Maccabees and the historian Josephus we learn that the Jewish upper classes of Judaea had forgotten the Torah, largely abandoned their Jewish practices, and embraced Hellenism, that is, Greek fashion, Greek religion and Greek thought. Even the High Priest, Menelaus, was leading a move to transform Jerusalem into a Greek city-state in order to make it eligible to stage the Olympic Games there. He was clearly untroubled by the fact that this would involve acts of worship to the Greek gods.

Like the Greeks, the young Jews were becoming obsessed with

212

their physical prowess, with keeping their bodies in peak condition, enabling them to compete in the *gymnasia*, while finding no time for worship of their own God, for study of His Torah and for developing their intellectual powers and their spiritual and moral sensitivity. Hence, before the main revolt against the Greeks, there was a prior struggle, led by that small band of loyal and pious Jews under Matityahu and Judah, that was directed against the internal assimilation of their Hellenized brethren. The Maccabees knew that they had no chance of defeating the Greeks until they had reversed the spiritual surrender of their own brethren to a foreign and idolatrous religion. Astonishingly, when the assimilated High Priest, Menelaus, saw that the Maccabees were about to seize Jerusalem, he called in the Greek-Syrians to help him repulse them. And hence the struggle widened into a full-scale, internal Jewish civil war.

So the core of the Chanukah saga was the struggle between Judaism and secular values for the hearts, souls and minds of the younger generation of Jews. And those who think that that struggle ended with the victory of the Maccabees are greatly mistaken. Because it is a struggle that is going on to this very day, and which has intensified in our age when most Jews naively and falsely seem to think that they cannot combine loyalty to their faith with success in the secular world, and that one cannot be an observant Jew and modern at the same time. The large number of Jewish Nobel prizewinners – totally disproportionate to our numbers – alone serves to explode that myth.

So this is one of the challenges of the Chanukah festival: to embrace the spirit and principles of the Maccabees, to be convinced, and to convince others, that success in life does not require surrender of one's cherished religious values and observances, but that, quite the contrary, one may gain much greater respect by being a multidimensional personality, with a strong, religious identity and a broader cultural and spiritual foundation to one's life.

CHAPTER SEVENTY-FOUR

Shabbat Zachor:
Remembering and proclaiming

Shabbat Zachor, 'The Shabbat of remembering', just before Purim, is the occasion to remember what the tyrant Amalek did to our people as they came out of Egypt, and how he inspired countless generations of his offspring to follow his cruel example.

To understand the scope of this word *zachor*, we need to consider an interesting feature underlying a large number of words in biblical Hebrew. Nearly all words in Hebrew carry their basic meaning within the three root letters that form their core. For this reason when we refer to a Hebrew verb we describe it in terms of just three letters: sh-m-r, 'to guard'; d-b-r, 'to speak'; b-n-h, 'to build'; and so on.

Now, there are some words in which the root letters actually interchange their positions. Hence we have the words *keves*, 'a lamb' (restaurant-goers will recall the course *keves batanur!*) and *kesev* (the identical letters interchanged), also meaning 'a lamb'. There is *simlah*, 'a garment' or 'dress', and *salmah*, with the identical meaning. Similarly, both the roots *gazar* and *garaz* mean 'to cut', 'to divide', from which we get the noun *garzen*, 'an axe'.

We can now appreciate another dimension of meaning that is associated with *Shabbat Zachor*, 'The Sabbath of Remembering.' And that is that it is not enough just to 'remember' — *zachor*. We also have to interchange those letters to ensure that we have taken account of all the nuances and shades of its meaning. Doing so, we discover two further roots, *karaz*, which means, 'to proclaim aloud', 'to declaim', and *kazar*, 'to be cruel' (from which come the nouns *achzar* (Deuteronomy 32: 33) and *achzari* (Proverbs, 12: 10) meaning 'cruel'.

The message here is clear: that we have to do far more than merely 'remember' (z-ch-r) the past, recalling how we were oppressed, exiled, cruelly persecuted (ch-z-r), and yet miraculously survived. If it is something we confine to the recesses of our collective memory or teach in the privacy of our homes or classes, then it has no constructive purpose.

Our past is not something merely 'to remember' (z-ch-r), but also 'to proclaim' (ch-r-z) with conviction each and every day of our life. We have to proclaim it by the dignified way we live our life, by the superior values we embrace, by the religious standards we set ourselves, by the spirituality we exude, and by the love of fellow man we demonstrate.

This duty of proclamation – of not suppressing our religious identity, but rather of promoting it every minute of every day – is contained in the first paragraph of the *Shema*, which states that God's

> words that I command you this day shall be in your heart. You shall impress them upon your children, and you shall speak of them when you sit at home and when you go on a journey, when you lie down and when you rise up ... *And you shall write them on the door-posts of your homes and upon your gates.*

In ancient times there could be no greater method of public proclamation than by writing a declaration on one's gate. Even today, important royal announcements, such as births, engagements and deaths, are posted up on the outside gates of Buckingham Palace. The duty of 'publicizing the miracle of Chanukah' originally involved lighting the festival lights outside, by the gates of the courtyard, and overlooking the public thoroughfare, so that as many passers-by as possible might witness the commemoration. Remembering is proclaiming. Similarly, cruelty (ch-z-r) has to be recalled (z-ch-r), proclaimed and exposed (ch-r-z), rooted out and purged.

This message of *Shabbat Zachor* is one that young people should especially take to heart. They should proclaim proudly their Jewish identity wherever they go, in word and by personal example, by the mitzvot they perform, the Torah they learn and teach, the people whose hearts they touch and whose minds they open.

CHAPTER SEVENTY-FIVE

Purim:
A time to speak out

There is a verse in Kohelet which states *eit lachashot v'eit ledabbeir,* 'There is a time to keep silent and a time to speak up' (3: 7). This verse could well have served as a sub-heading to the Book of Esther which relates the dilemma that Esther faced as to whether or not to speak up, whether or not to acknowledge that she was a Jewess, whether or not to declare her relationship to Mordechai, whether or not to disclose to the king at the outset the identity of the man who was plotting to destroy her people, whether or not to go to the king uninvited to speak up and plead her people's cause, whether or not to tell the king at the first banquet what her motive was in inviting Haman. Esther was clearly very reticent to speak out. She appreciated the need for diplomacy, for selecting the right moment of maximum impact, for knowing the 'time to keep silent and the time to speak out'.

There was once a trial in a small town somewhere in the deep South of the USA. The prosecution lawyer called his first witness to the stand – an elderly great-grandma who had lived in the town for eighty years and knew all its inhabitants from birth. The lawyer approached her and asked, 'Mrs Jones, do you know me?'

'Of course, Mr Thomas', she responded. 'I've known you since you were a whipper-snapper, and you haven't changed one iota. You were a loud-mouthed trouble-making liar, a manipulator and a cheat, then, and you haven't changed!'

The lawyer was stunned. Not knowing what else to do, he pointed across the room and asked, 'Mrs Jones, do you know my learned friend, the defence attorney?'

'Of course I do', she replied with a wicked smile. 'And he's far from learned. He's lazy, bigoted, and he has a gambling and drink problem. He can't build a normal relationship with anyone and his law practice is one of the worst in the entire state. He was born a loser, and he still is.' The defence lawyer went white.

The judge then summoned the prosecution lawyer to approach his bench, and in a very quiet but firm voice, said, 'If you dare ask her if she knows me, I'll throw you in jail for contempt!'

That lady's careless speech was in sharp contrast to the cautious, diplomatic approach taken by Queen Esther in the Megillah.

There is a passage in the sidrah Vayikra (Leviticus 5:1) which deals with this same issue of speaking out in the cause of truth. Interestingly, the verb it uses is the identical one employed by the Book of Esther when dealing with that same issue. There we read that if a person is a witness but withholds his evidence and does not speak up, he is guilty of a serious sin.

The Hebrew term used for withholding evidence is im lo yagid ('if he will not disclose'), and that is the identical verb (le-hagid) as used in the Megillah to describe Esther's withholding of information regarding her Jewish identity: Ein Esther magedet moladtah v'al amah, 'Esther did not disclose her land of origin or her people'.

Over the past decades we Jews have been thrown on the defensive as our enemies, at home, in the Middle East and around the world, have attempted to silence and intimidate us, to condemn us in the United Nations, and to force Israel to make concessions without the guarantee of peace in return. They camouflage their hatred of Jews by attacking Israel and blaming her for the violence and turbulence in the Middle East. They deny her the right to defend herself and have more sympathy for the death of terrorists than innocent Israeli citizens. Right-wing groups deny or play down the Holocaust, launch attacks on Jews, synagogues and Jewish communal buildings, and propose a steady stream of anti-Israel motions on university campuses, making life very tense there for Jewish students.

The dearest wish of our enemies, the modern day Hamans, is to intimidate us into silence. But the message of the Torah's denunciation of a witness who refuses to testify, and of Mordechai's sharp denunciation of Esther for attempting to keep a low profile and hold her peace, is that we must stand strong, united and courageous, and, when the moment demands it, we must speak out, loudly, with conviction and with authority, declaring our support for *ammeinu umoladteinu*, our people and our land, and vindicate the justice of Israel's cause.

It is upon the ranks of the younger generation that our people will have to rely to represent our cause to the nations and to continue the struggle against anti-Semitism. We pray desperately that things will change, and they will be blessed to live in Kohelet's *eit lachashot*, a period when they will no longer need to speak out in the defence of their people. But at the moment it is definitely *eit ledabbeir*, 'a time to speak out', when we expect our young people to be our spokesmen and spokeswomen.

CHAPTER SEVENTY-SIX

Purim:
A minor festival with
a major message

Purim commemorates the release of the Jews from the grip of those forces that sought their destruction in the ancient Persian Empire. How did the Jews respond to the threat that had faced them and the victory they achieved? Most nations in antiquity who suffered as we Jews did determined that they would never become victims again. So they invested vast sums of money into their defence, developing sophisticated weapons of war, increasing the size of their army, training specialist commando units, placing the emphasis on being able to match violence with greater violence.

The Jew was taught a quite different approach to oppression, hatred and war. He was taught to meet hostility with an extra measure of love and concern for fellow man. He was conditioned to eradicate evil by building a more caring society that would become a model for the more warlike to follow, so that the spirit of violence would be diminished in the world. The Jew celebrated victory not by glorying in his strength, but by giving Mishloach manot (gifts to friends) – demonstrating the superior power of friendship, peace and harmony – and matanot la'evyonim (charitable support to the less fortunate).

Most nations, when they celebrated anniversaries of great military victories, emphasized only the heroism, and the genius of the military tactics and initiatives employed. They played down the fear that had gripped the country, the prayers directed to God and the sacrifices made by ordinary folk.

We Jews have a unique way of responding to life's situations; and we learned how to do so from the most unexpected sources and rituals. Those little things we do on Purim are an example of profound teachings couched in terms of simple religious acts. And the fact that, as a prelude to Purim, we have always observed and commemorated the Fast of Esther, demonstrating just how weak and vulnerable we were, and how totally reliant on God's mercy, is a classic example of just how we have always credited God, not ourselves, with being the source of all our victories, good fortune and blessings.

The Torah's laws and teachings can transform not only a person but also the world itself. They teach us humility, and how to believe in ourselves while putting our ultimate trust in God.

CHAPTER SEVENTY-SEVEN

Is Haman foreshadowed
in the Torah?

The Talmudic sages believed that there was nothing in Jewish history, or, indeed, in life itself, that could not be traced back to, or read into, the text of the Torah. It is as if the Torah contains a kind of comprehensive genetic or forensic blueprint that could be tapped into to provide information not only about the period that the Torah covers, but also about any subsequent period throughout Jewish history.

From this perspective, it is not strange that the Talmud should have asked the question, *Haman min ha-Torah minnayin*, 'Where is there a reference to Haman in the Torah?' (Tal. Hullin 139b) – even though Haman lived about 900 years after the Torah was given!

If the question is not strange, the answer certainly is. The Talmud responds that a reference to Haman occurs in the earliest story of Adam and Eve, when God says to Adam, *Hamin ha'eitz asher tziviticha* ... "Did you eat from the fruit that I warned you against eating?" (Genesis 3: 11). The lively imagination of the rabbis thus made a direct association between the words *Hamin* and *Haman*. (That the vowels 'i' and 'a' interchange may be demonstrated by the fact that the early Bible translators rendered the Hebrew name Bilaam as Balaam.) It was certainly with tongue in cheek that they made that suggestion that the earliest biblical story of Adam and Eve was already programmed with a linking word (*Hamin*) in order to foreshadow the Purim story!

Now, if we left that Talmudic idea without elucidation most of us would scratch our head and wrinkle up our brow, because it begs the question why the Torah would have planted that reference to Haman just in the story of Adam and Eve? What possible connection could there be between those two stories?

The answer I would suggest is that both episodes depict an identical character flaw, namely the tendency to become obsessed with what one is missing rather than to rejoice in the blessings we possess.

Take the story of Adam and Eve. They were placed in the most beautiful garden in the world, where they had absolutely everything they needed. Every single variety of tree, fruit and vegetable was theirs to enjoy as and when they wanted. There were no pressures, no struggle to earn a livelihood. Life was idyllic. There was just the little matter of a solitary tree that God had prohibited.

What did Eve do? She banished from her mind all those countless blessings, and she became totally obsessed with, and depressed by, the one single tree that was out of bounds. Nothing else tasted sweet as long as she could not enjoy that forbidden fruit.

If we examine the story of Haman we find the identical syndrome. Haman had everything: a beautiful wife and home, ten sons, wealth, power, the highest office in the state, the acclaim and adulation of everyone in the 127 provinces of Media and Persia. Was he satisfied? Was he able to sit back and enjoy all the fruits of his labours? No he was not.

Why not? Because there happened to be a Jew – one single Jew in the context of the several million people that comprised the 127 provinces of Media and Persia – who did not follow the herd, and who refused to bow down when he passed by. Haman could not focus on what he had – on the millions who acclaimed him. Instead he was fixated by one individual Jew who was the exception to the rule.

Now we can understand what the Talmudic rabbis meant when they asked where Haman was alluded to in the Torah. They were really asking where in the Torah we find a precedent for the Haman-obsession with what one was missing, rather than the blessings in abundance that one possessed. And their answer was that, at the very beginning of the Torah, in the Garden of Eden, we already encounter that same misguided ingratitude, that tendency which, at a later period, in Persia, would be so acute as to prompt a Haman to attempt to slaughter an entire people on the altar of his own pride and vainglory.

Young people are stepping out into a world of consumerism where they are bombarded on all sides by adverts that seek to convince them that they are missing out on so many things that are vital to the quality of their lives. Newspapers and magazines, radio and television channels and giant-sized advertisement hoardings, are all jam-packed with offers that are too good to be true, with fantastic claims being made for the latest diets, pills and cosmetics. They hold out exaggerated claims to make people appear younger, healthier and more beautiful than they are, and they offer investments that promise instant wealth. They persuade the gullible that they absolutely must have updates for the 'old-fashioned' products that they bought but a few months before. They convince both those who can and cannot afford it that true happiness in life is unattainable without the most expensive luxuries.

The number of gullible people overwhelmed by debt that they can never repay, that they have accumulated through irresponsible spending and by believing the hype and the lies that the advertising industry has fed them on, is growing alarmingly year by year. These are the people who have been induced to focus exclusively on what they do not have, and to devalue what they have.

Our Ethics of the Fathers says, *Eizehu ashiyr? ha-sameach b'chelko*, 'Who is really wealthy? He who is content with what he has' (4: 1). So few people are content with what they have. Few really count their blessings. They are too busy dreaming of greater, more expensive, more valuable and more satisfying blessings. Too many people define blessings in terms of objects, rather than in terms of people.

The real blessings are the family we have, the good friends we cultivate, the mitzvot, the good deeds, we accumulate, the good name we achieve, the kindnesses we dispense, the cheerfulness we exude, and the love, peace and harmony that we foster all around.

And nowhere is this emphasized more than in the final verse of the Book of Esther. In many ways it is an astonishing climax to the story of the terrible struggle of the Jews of Persia against their enemies. Mordechai had led this struggle with great personal heroism. Almost single-handedly he had mustered the courage to oppose and unmask the cruel and influential Prime Minister, Haman, and had led the campaign to frustrate all Haman's plans and to lead the Jews in a lightning battle, culminating in a most amazing victory over their enemies throughout the empire and particularly in Shushan, the very heart of government and military administration.

The book understandably ends with a citation in praise of Mordechai. We might have expected some reference to all that courage and bravery on the field of battle. Instead, what is the crowning achievement with which it credits him? It is this:

Ki Mordechai ha-yehudiy mishneh lamelech Achashverosh – 'For Mordechai the Jew became second in rank to King Achashverosh' ... gadol la-yehudim v'ratzui l'rov echav – 'great among the Jews and popular among the ranks of his brethren' ... doreish tov l'ammo v'doveir shalom lechol zar'o – 'seeking the good of his people and promoting the welfare of all their descendants' (Esther 10: 3).

Mordechai's real achievement lay not in his prowess as a brave commander and leader, and certainly not in the personal fame, wealth, power and influence that he gained by reason of becoming second in rank to the king. It lay rather in the giving of himself wholeheartedly to the service of his brethren. He was ratzui, 'beloved' of them; he was doreish tov, 'ever seeking their good'; he was doveir shalom, 'a promoter of peace', patching up quarrels, restoring strained relationships. He spent all his remaining years, not sitting back and enjoying his state pension, but in the service of his people.

Mordechai serves as an inspirational hero and role model, guiding us to focus always on the blessings we have, rather than on those we have failed to acquire. He challenges us all to find our fulfilment and joy in sharing our blessings with the less fortunate of our people, in promoting the welfare of our community and, like him, in creating peace and harmony among all those with whom we come into contact.

CHAPTER SEVENTY-EIGHT

A *Parashat Ha-Chodesh* Bar/Bat Mitzvah: The first month of your new life

The special Maftir portion for *Parashat Ha-Chodesh* deals with the various laws and rituals that the Israelites were commanded to observe as part of the celebratory meal of the Paschal lamb which they ate prior to their exodus from Egypt. The contents of the Maftir section are known better than those of any other Maftir in the whole Torah. This is, simply, because they are the details of the Passover Seder. And no one who retains any sense of Jewish identity absents himself from that religious celebration.

So, because everyone is so fully informed on this subject we shall not address the subjects of Paschal Lamb, the matzah, maror or any other of those familiar elements, but rather provide a simple message derived from an apparently unnecessary repetition in the very opening verse of the Maftir.

It commences, *Ha-chodesh ha-zeh lachem rosh chodashim* – ('This month shall be for you as the beginning of the months') – *rishon hu lachem l'chodshei hashanah* ('It shall be the first for you of the months of the year').

The simple explanation of this overemphasis is that, until this moment the Israelites had observed the month of Tishri as the first month, which is why Rosh Hashanah, the new year, is on the first of that month. Truly, that was the more logical month with which to begin a new agricultural year, for that was the time when the farmer hoed his land and planted his seed before the onset of winter. That was the case while the Israelites lived in Goshen and possessed rich lands to cultivate and on which to pasture their flocks. But at the dawn of the Exodus two factors emerged to prompt the new

226

year to be moved to the month of Nisan. The first was the fact that the Israelites became a new sovereign nation in Nisan when they achieved their freedom and left Egypt. The second factor was that, because of their sin, they were destined to be detained for a lengthy stay of forty years in the desert when they would have no fields to cultivate. Thus, there was no point in having an agricultural 'new year'. Hence it was far more logical to suspend the counting from Tishri, and instead celebrate Nisan, when they gained their independence, as the first month of their 'civil year.'

And now we can understand why the Torah over-emphasized the word *lachem*, 'for you'. Until now, your ancestors had a different new year, but because of your special destiny, this particular month of Nisan will now become *your* new year, the first of the months of *your* year.

Against this background we may appreciate why this is such a relevant Maftir for a Bar or Bat Mitzvah, since this month is also the first month of their Jewish adulthood. They gain their religious independence from this month on, and their freedom to determine what sort of Jew they are going to be. They have to make their own choice. And hopefully it will be to opt for the Torah way. The word *lachem*, 'for you' thus has a special resonance. From this month on it is no longer their parents' responsibility to ensure that they keep the mitzvot. It is their own decision, reflected in the father's blessing after his son has been called to the Torah on his Bar Mitzvah: *Baruch shep'tarani mei'onsho shel zeh*, 'Blessed be God who has now relieved me of [religious] responsibility for my son'.

There is one authority, R. Baruch Ha-Levi Epstein, who states that the father of girls should also recite that formula – *Baruch shep'tarani mei'onsho shel zo't* – on the day their daughters attain Bat Mitzvah. So the Torah, in effect, says to every Bar and Bat Mitzvah *Ha-chodesh ha-zeh* **lachem** *rosh chodashim*, 'This month is for you the first of all the months of the new religious life that is ahead of you'. *Rishon hu* **lachem** *lechodshei ha-shanah* – 'It is your challenge to make every month of every year truly *lachem*, your own, suffused with your special talents and qualities, your own religious enthusiasm, your own expressions of loyalty to your faith and your people, your own particular contribution to your synagogue and your community.'

227

CHAPTER SEVENTY-NINE

Pesach's call to all young adults

Pesach is the festival of Jewish identity. It marked the point of transition for Jacob's offspring, who began as a family, grew into a clan, then expanded, amid the Egyptian period of slavery, into a nation. It then further evolved, through the Exodus and the Giving of the Torah, into the Chosen People, chosen to live by the most exacting moral standards, to be God-like in their concern for struggling humanity, and to bring ethical civilization to the ancient, and indeed the modern, world.

There are many people who think that modern society is so much more enlightened than that of antiquity or of the so-called Dark Ages. Nothing could be further from the truth. Man may have far greater technological skills, such as instantaneous means of communication, bringing news and entertainment into his living room, but, as far as his character is concerned, man has not changed one iota. His nature is the same. His aggression, his greed, his desire for power, his suspicion of the stranger, his ability to nurse a grievance for decades, and a prejudice, such as against Jews, for 2,000 years. The one thing that modern society has indeed perfected is the art of killing people with weapons of mass destruction, which the ancients could never have achieved.

Pesach is the festival which, above all, preaches love, inclusiveness, peace and respect for all ages and for all peoples. The Jew cannot feel secure or content as long as there are other oppressed and poverty-stricken people in the world. The Torah tells us that, while we were enslaved in Egypt, there was an *eirev rav*, a vast mixed multitude of ethnic groups and enslaved foreigners who had been sold into slavery there and deprived of their rights (Exodus 12: 38). When the moment of Israelite liberation arrived, we are told that our ancestors insisted on liberating and escorting out of Egypt that vast oppressed foreign entity. That is what Judaism is about: practical and charitable concern for all mankind. It is clear, in our unfeeling world, that the Jewish mission has not yet run its course.

In addition to tolerance and concern for other peoples, Pesach also addresses the quality of the relationship that is expected within the narrower confines of one's family and immediate circle. The troubles of our people in Egypt first began with the brothers' jealousy of Joseph and their sale of him into slavery. The battles within one family thus had tragic repercussions on a vast national scale that they could never have imagined.

But how could such destructive behaviour ever be redeemed and removed from the record? Only by a powerful corresponding demonstration of love and tolerance towards people who were alien to the Israelite people, in their behaviour and temperament, and unequal in their intellect, but whose humanity alone might serve as the bridge between the Israelites and them. Hence the slavery was caused by internal hatred, and it came to an end with a powerful demonstration of external concern exhibited towards the members of 'the mixed multitude'. The slavery began with people treating their brothers as strangers, and ended with them treating strangers as brothers.

In that spirit, the Haggadah insists that all those diverse members of a family, all the parties to any potential conflict, must be brought to sit around the same Seder table. The wise and committed son next to the wicked, defiant one; and the simple son, who does not clearly comprehend the purpose and value of faith, next to the doubly simple son who doesn't even *want* to know about it, and whose total indifference prevents him framing a single question.

There is a place in the Jewish home, in the Jewish family, in the Jewish heart, for all our sons, however interested or disinterested they may be, however learned or ignorant they may be. Indeed, a famous Chasidic teacher, the Seer of Lublin once said: 'I prefer a wicked person who knows he is a sinner; than an observant person who thinks that he is righteous.'

Pesach calls upon all young adults to feel themselves as indispensable parts of the Jewish community whether their knowledge of Judaism is great or little, whether their level of observance is high or low, and to determine to extend friendship and concern to all their brethren, to the very best of their ability.

CHAPTER EIGHTY

Pesach and open-minded enquiry

Pesach invites all young adults to maintain the eager quest for knowledge and the thirst for authentic answers that form the very structure of the Seder. The Seder is a child-orientated event, giving the four categories of children ample scope to ask their questions, even to express their doubts and criticisms of the community and its commitment: *Mah zot?* – 'What is this for?'; *Mah ha-eidut v'hachukim v'hamishpatim* – 'Why do you need all those detailed regulations?'; *Mah ha'avodah hazot lachem* – 'What do you gain from all this ritual?'

I do not believe there is any other religion that gives such freedom of expression, to doubt and to criticize, as does Judaism. One faith burned doubters or critics on the stake, instituted an Inquisition to seek out, punish and mutilate such renegades. And another major religion issued *fatwas*, encouraging the faithful to take the law into their own hands, and kill those who were critical of the religion or its adherents.

Judaism believes in open dialogue. It welcomes the spirit of free enquiry as a challenge. It never stifles or suppresses argument. It never coerces. It debates. It throws up its own objections in the honest search for ultimate answers. The entire Talmudic method is to stockpile principles, concepts and ideas, and to subject them to a rigorous critical analysis.

Judaism encourages curiosity. It is never offended by honest doubters and it is as content to welcome the *rasha*, the wicked son, to the Seder, as it is to welcome the *chakham*, the wise son.

And this is another message of this festival. The penultimate verse of the haftarah for Shabbat Ha-Gadol, the Shabbat before Pesach, refers to the coming of Elijah the Prophet. In our tradition, we accept that we do not have all the answers, that some elements of faith and observance may remain unclear or even problematic. Elijah is the one who, when he arrives to usher in the Messianic age, will first address all those difficult questions. He will provide the definitive answers. He will reveal the hidden mysteries, solve all the problems and satisfy all the doubters. Our task, however, in the meantime, is to see how much we can learn, how many of the problems we can solve, and how much light we can shed on our ancient texts.

That is the challenge of this period to all our young adults. That is the approach of the wise son. *Tzei ulmad*, 'Go and learn!'

Index